A Global View of Financial Accounting

A Global View of Financial Accounting

Roger Hussey and Talal Al-Hayale

BEP

BUSINESS EXPERT PRESS

Leader in applied, concise business books

A Global View of Financial Accounting

Copyright © Business Expert Press, LLC, 2022.

Cover design by Charlene Kronstedt

Interior design by Exeter Premedia Services Private Ltd., Chennai, India

First published in 2022 by
Business Expert Press, LLC
222 East 46th Street, New York, NY 10017
www.businessexpertpress.com

ISBN-13: 978-1-63742-283-0 (paperback)
ISBN-13: 978-1-63742-284-7 (e-book)

Business Expert Press Financial Accounting Collection

First edition: 2022

10 9 8 7 6 5 4 3 2 1

Description

Different types of measurement are parts of our life and, to a large extent, they have a consistency. The measurement of time and temperature remains the same regardless of country and circumstances. Time raises some issues when we are making international comparisons because of the shape of the world. It may be 8.00 a.m. in Australia but different in the United Kingdom and the United States. There are also differences because some countries insist on certain dates in the year to "put the clocks back/forward" for an hour. Somewhat annoying, but we have learnt to live with it. Measuring temperature also has significant consistency with some countries measuring in Celsius and others in Fahrenheit, but the translation from one to the other is consistent.

Length, weight, and distance also have different country methods but are translatable. If you buy a piece of wood in the United Kingdom that is six feet long, then the next six feet piece of wood will be the same length as the first. If you are measuring it in the United States, it will be meters or centimeters. It will be exactly the same physical length as the UK purchase but we use different terms for measurement. The same rules apply to weight and distance. These measurements have a consistency and we can "translate" them easily into another currency.

When we come to measuring value, the position is very different both within one country and in comparing to other countries. The length of our wood can stay the same but the price of the wood may vary because financial measurement does not have the same consistency. The cost of the wood can increase and decrease depending on several factors and also change from one country to another. The result is when we come to the measurement of financial transactions, we need guidance on the best method; otherwise recipients of the information will not be able to understand it.

Unfortunately, the reality of measuring in monetary terms has major issues even when measuring in the same currency. Costs and selling prices of items change for a variety of reasons. To resolve this issue for accounting transactions, countries have set standards on how accounting transactions should be calculated. This does not stop costs fluctuating but, at least, we understand how the calculation has been made. Unfortunately, at the international level, we do not have complete agreement on how to calculate cost and there are different approaches. In this book, we explore those financial transactions where accounting rules have attempted to resolve this inconsistency basis and we identify the differences on a country basis.

Keywords

financial accounting standards board; international accounting standards board; islamic accounting; securities and exchange commission; sharia law; sustainability; zakat

Contents

CHAPTER 1

Financial Measurements

Introduction

There has always been the preoccupation for valuing objects and human activities. If we measure or weigh any object, we have specific data that are reliable, unless circumstances change and that is the problem. A 20-meter length of wood will always be 20 meters and weigh the same amount. However, the cost of it will fluctuate depending on several factors. Accounting relies on financial measurement to determine the value of objects and the performance of companies. Unfortunately, the concept of monetary value can depend on the circumstances. Water in the desert is worth much—a burst water pipe in your kitchen is a pain.

In this chapter, we examine first the problems in identifying and recording business transactions. For several centuries, this preoccupation with identifying the monetary value of items and activities was unresolved. The method for recording business transactions also presented challenges until the advent of double-entry bookkeeping. This brief review of history is followed by a discussion of the concepts accountants now use to attempt to bring validity and consistency to the information they generate. We then explain the dilemma on whether accountants should follow strict rules in conducting their work or is the application of basic principles more useful. The final section before our conclusions looks at the very important, and still unresolved, issue of the impact of inflation on identifying, measuring, and recording financial transactions.

What Do We Want?

The How and the Why

Most books you read on recording financial information spend most of the time on the "How" and very little on the "Why." This results in very detailed and informative books on accounting procedures and methods (the How), often referred to as accounting standards. But if you do not know the reasons for recording the information (the Why), you have no guide as to the amount and type of information to be included. We can suggest various possibilities for the use of information.

To manage an organization. Financial accounting is the term that is usually used for identifying and recording business transactions. The information can be used to report to various people and organizations the activities of a business. However, such information is not useful for managing large organizations on a daily basis. For this activity, we need to use a separate discipline called management accounting. This specifically sets out methods for collecting financial information and describes various methods and techniques for managing an organization.

To calculate the taxes required by the government. Not the most rewarding exercise and not acceptable by itself for regular management information. Most countries have their own tax regulations, which differ from the financial accounting regulations. A certain amount of adjustments have to be made to the calculated profit using financial accounting regulations to arrive at a figure that is acceptable to the tax authorities.

To enable not-for-profit organizations to continue their work. These organizations provide support for various members of the community and rely on donations to do this. The funding raised by them can be very large. For example, the U.S. charity "Feeding America" noted in its 2020 Annual Report that the total public support and revenue for that year was $3.6 billion. The financial statements of the organization have been properly audited and the auditors state that they comply with "the accounting principles generally accepted in the United States." Note that the auditors refer to the country and that is because different countries can have different accounting practices. These international differences can be frustrating, and we explain in Chapter 2 the present position.

To inform the owners or financial contributors of a "for-profit" organization. Understandably, owners may consider that calculating their profit is possibly the best reason for having accounting regulations and recording financial transactions in an appropriate way. However, there are different types of organizations conducting different types of business from manufacturing articles to offering a service. There may also be different types of owners or participants requiring different financial information.

To overcome the issue of the various organizations and their financial disclosures, it is easiest when establishing financial accounting regulations in a country to identify and focus on the business entity. The underlying concept considers that the business is separate from the owner(s) and the purpose of the entity is to make a profit. Financial statements are prepared to reflect the activities of the business and not the owners. Although the concept is simple, there are intercountry differences and some examples where "special" business entities exist. These will be explained later in this chapter.

The Business Entity or the Organization or the Company...

In this book, for simplicity, we use the term business entity and this encompasses any type of organization whose main purpose is to make a profit. This means that we are not including such organizations as charities, government agencies, and social clubs, which have their own regulatory requirements. In this book, it is assumed that the business is separate from the owner(s), with the actual business and its owners being treated as two separately identifiable parties. Financial statements are prepared to reflect the activities of the business and not the owners.

There have been several attempts in the United States to define clearly the meaning of "business entity." One committee (Concepts and Standards Research Study Committee) in 1964 concluded that, in discussing underlying concepts, the term "business entity" was unnecessarily restrictive, if not misleading. The underlying concept is identical whether the area of economic interest being accounted for is a business, a nonprofit organization, governmental unit, or any other form of economic activity. The committee recommended, therefore, that the underlying concept be referred to as the entity concept. In this book, we are concentrating on "business entities" which are considered profit making, but some of the material we provide is also relevant for colleges and universities, municipalities, nonprofit hospitals, charitable foundations, and all other classes of "economic entities."

We recommend readers to use the term which is most prevalent in their own country. In reading or compiling financial statements, it is useful to think of the business as an "entity" separated completely from the owner or owners. Entities listed on a stock exchange are frequently labeled as groups, that is, a number of separate companies either wholly owned or partly owned by a holding company. As users of financial statements, we are usually interested in seeing the financial statements for the group and that is our reporting or business entity.

Double the Work

This section of the chapter starts with a disclaimer. We have selected from the many writings on accounting history, those aspects that contribute to our main theme of corporate financial reporting by business entities, but it is argued that such an approach lacks "the depth of knowledge and critical appreciation that a specialist historian of accounting will bring to the exposition of history" (Carnegie and Napier 2013). We accept that criticism but for those readers who wish to delve deeper into the history of money, there are numerous books and reviews such as Hancock, Sprague, and Scott (1912) and, more recently by, Schneider, Morys, Lampe, and Enflo (2017).

Having made the above disclaimer, it is useful to give some historical foundation to better understand the current thinking on financial measurement and recording for business entities. Our discussion starts with the earliest period of a form of recording. The desire to know the "value" of things you own or control and the practice of recording that information has been with us for many centuries. To enable the exchange of goods and services, people have used numerous commodities such as tobacco in Colonial Virginia, sugar in the West Indies, salt in Abyssinia, cows in Ancient Greece, nails in Scotland, copper in Ancient Egypt, and also grains, tea, animal skins, fish hooks, and other items.

The move from the use of various commodities to a coinage system has been detailed by William and Hansen (2013). They argue that there were several stages that commenced in Sumeria. Government officials developed clay tokens of various geometric shapes and patterns, with one token equaling one measure of grain. They realized that if a mark on a clay tablet could represent a specific good, then a second mark could represent a quantity of goods. Between 1400 and 1500 AD, a third significant abstraction occurred. Standard coinage had appeared throughout Europe. Countries minted their own coinage but also recognized currency values of different nations, thus goods could be assigned a monetary value. Instead of an accounting transaction being recorded in units of wheat, the actual cost of wheat, expressed in a currency, was now recorded. This third stage solved a valuation or comparability argument and allowed resources and obligations to be expressed in a homogenous manner based on currency representations. In other words, we need conformity in keeping records and when reporting financial transactions.

Unfortunately, currencies are subject to a multitude of external and internal environmental factors that affect their extrinsic values. These factors relate to physical and cultural variables. The simple passage of time combined with inflationary pressures alters the purchasing power of currencies and the assumption of homogenous properties. For example, 5 francs may equal 1 dollar, but will 5 francs equal 1 dollar a few years, or even weeks, from now? Even in accounts of an entity within a specific culture, would a dollar today equal a future dollar? Thus, the third abstraction of currency representation creates a variety of measuring complexities. As Taggart (1953) points out, the concept of measurement using the assumption of a stable homogenous dollar as a measuring unit raises problems. The amount identified does not have the same purchasing power over time and it is misleading to users of financial information for accountants to add or subtract dollars spent at different times. The problem is fully acknowledged by accountants, but a solution to resolve this has not been found. We discuss the debate and the issues in the final section of this chapter.

The issue of changing values over time is recognized, but it has not influenced the method of recording monetary transactions and identifying values. All students spend significant time wrestling with the technique of recording financial transactions known as double-entry bookkeeping. Remember that clever as it is, the purpose of the method is to ensure that accounting transactions are properly recorded. The terms double entry and dual entry are used somewhat loosely for the method for recording transactions, but Sangster (2016) states that the difference between dual entry and double entry lies in how the contra entry is recorded. In double entry, each entry in an account must include the location of the account in which the contra entry has been made. No such information is provided in dual entry.

The term double entry will always be associated with the Franciscan friar and teacher of mathematics Luca Pacioli, who in 1494 published an instructional treatise describing the system of double-entry bookkeeping. It is claimed (Sangster 2018) that Pacioli's teaching method was inspired by Euclid, his Franciscan education, and his humanist beliefs. This may not influence current students' passion, or lack of it, for bookkeeping but, if transactions are properly recorded, it is possible to construct financial statements. These, however, are the output from a recording method and not an attempt at valuation. The following short example demonstrates the valuation issues which nobody has been able to resolve satisfactorily.

Example of Double-Entry Bookkeeping

Period 1

Company purchases 3,000 roles of product A at $50 per role = $150,000

Total labor costs for preparing the roles for sale = $50,000

The 3,000 roles are then sold for $80 per role = $240,000

Profit for the period (sales minus costs) = $40,000

Period 2

The same number and type of roles are purchased and sold but there are some changes. The general rate of inflation is 10 percent for the roles and the employees have bargained for a rise of 15 percent and the company has managed to increase the price it charges by $8 per role.

The financial results for period 2 are:

The selling price is set at $88 per role for 3,000 roles.

Sales of roles at $88 per role being the price at which transactions can be made = $264,000

The cost of the roles is increased to $55 per role (the inflated cost) = $165,000

Total labor costs = $57,500

Profit for the period = $41,500

One could conclude from the profit figures that the company is showing financial improvements this period compared to the previous one. However, in practical terms, nothing has changed with the basic activities of the company. It is producing and selling the same number of roles. Investors may conclude that their profit has increased by $4,000, but there have been significant changes. The costs have increased but, by increasing the selling price, the company has increased profit. But the activity level is static with only 3,000 roles in both periods.

In real life, it is unlikely that the selling price, labor costs, and material costs will all increase by 10 percent. It is probable that there will be variations. The labor costs may increase to $60,000 due to labor shortages and the need to attract employees. Material costs may have declined and an increase in the selling price may have reduced the numbers sold. The financial statements do not provide this information. We have not included noncurrent assets such as the property that is occupied and the machinery that is used. In all probability, the property would have increased in value and the machinery would have been depreciated by an arbitrary amount.

Double-entry bookkeeping ensures that the transactions are recorded but they do not necessarily reflect changes in the level of activity and the changes in costs due to increases in property values and decreases due to inflation. The answer, of course, is to apply financial measures that recognize these changes. As we discuss later in this chapter, when we consider the subject of the principles versus rules to financial accounting, this has proved very difficult.

From Recording to Reporting

Recording Financial Transactions

The purpose of recording financial transactions is to provide a record that can be examined by someone who wishes to understand the activities of the organization. Many years ago, the owner of a business may have been the only user of the financial information and would need to record financial transactions to manage the business. Undoubtedly, tax authorities would also be interested in the financial transactions. As businesses became larger and more complex, the number of those interested in

financial information became larger and they may have been legally entitled to receive it. It is the role of the accountant to meet these information
needs. In doing so, the accountant will not only be dealing with facts but
also be compelled to make certain estimates and will follow various concepts and assumptions.

Many years ago, accountants had considerable flexibility in deciding
how to treat various issues, and the requirements of the local tax authority frequently established some rules. As business became more complicated, there was a need for countries, or the accounting profession or
other regulators in a country, to publish guidelines and advice for keeping
accounting records. There needed to be confidence in the financial information and the various users required the reassurance that all users had
similar information. For example, all accountants in a particular country accounted for financial transactions and events in a similar way. This
meant that the users of the financial statements could understand the
basis on which the statements had been prepared and be able to compare
the financial results of one organization with another in the same country.

Users of Financial Information

So far in this chapter, we have discussed the process of accounting and the
concepts and assumptions that accountants use in preparing periodic financial statements. We will complete this chapter by explaining the purpose
of preparing financial statements and the possible users of financial statements. Before that, we provide the framework for our discussions by using
as a guide the requirements as set out in the Conceptual Framework with
revisions in International Accounting Standards (IASs) 1, *Presentation of
Financial Statements*, effective from 1 January 2005. Conceptual Frameworks have been issued by various accounting regulators and the purpose
is to establish consistent rules and standards for preparing financial statements. A lengthier approach to the subject than the IAS is the U.S. Financial Accounting Standard Board's (FASB) *Accounting Standards Codification*.

The Conceptual Framework issued by the International Accounting
Standards Board (IASB) explains that it is concerned only with general-purpose financial statements. These statements are prepared and presented at least annually by companies to meet the common information

needs of a wide range of users. We would emphasize that the tax authorities in most countries have their own methods for determining the taxable profit. Two objectives of general-purpose financial statements are
identified.

1. To provide information about the financial position, performance,
   and changes in financial position that is useful in making economic
   decisions
2. To show the results of the stewardship of management or the
   accountability of management for the resources entrusted to it

There are generally considered to be two main needs for user of financial information. These are usually referred to as the decision model and
the stewardship model. To a large extent, they are incompatible and it is
extremely difficult to prepare general-purpose financial statements that
achieve both objectives. To explain the arguments, we will summarize
them into two extreme viewpoints although there are various ranges
of opinion.

It is argued that the decision model must provide information that is
relevant and the most interested users would be the providers of capital,
that is, those who financially support the company—shareholders and
lenders. The purpose of financial statements is to assist them in making
decisions regarding their financial dealings with a company. Advocates of
the stewardship model contend that what is most important is the reliability of the information and that there is a moral, if not a legal, obligation for entities to provide information to a wide range of users who may
be interested in its activities, current employees being a good example.
There has also been growing pressure for companies to provide additional
information, such as their impact on the environment. We discuss these
issues in Chapter 5.

There is a conflict between the objectives of information being relevant
to the users' needs and the reliability of the information. This impacts on
the method of measurement you use, particularly for items on the balance
sheet. If you follow the stewardship model, you would attempt to make
the information to be extremely reliable and traditionally accountants
have used the historical cost concept. Applying this concept, there are no

adjustments made for changes in the value of money. If you purchased land 20 years ago for $200,000, it will still remain at that figure in your financial statements. The alternative model of decision usefulness requires the information to be relevant to decisions you are making now, which means that the value of assets must be their present value and not the historical cost that may be 50 years out of date.

In the above example, we used the example of land and one can assume that land usually increases in value, but how do we account for the other assets held by the company. A manufacturing company will have a substantial investment in machinery, which is likely to lose its value the longer it is used. It is usual practice to depreciate these assets over a period of years. This is only a mathematical approach and not an attempt at valuation.

This debate on valuation of assets has been around for many decades and there has been a move away from historical cost accounting to various methods for measuring current values. This has led to heated discussions on the different methods used for current valuations, their reliability or lack of it, and the unintended consequences on the financial performance and position of companies in various economic climates.

We will discuss these issues in subsequent chapters, but an agreement has been very difficult to achieve, particularly on an international basis. There are different opinions on who the users of financial statements are, or should be, and on the information they need, and we discuss these issues in Chapter 2. At this stage, we examine the many potential users of company financial statements with their differing information needs and discuss these below.

Shareholders

There are three basic types of decisions taken by shareholders who invest in a company. They wish to know whether to buy more shares, hold on to shares they already own, or sell part or all of the shares they own. In making these decisions, the investor will not only be considering the potential future of an individual company but the prospects for the stock market. In trying to predict the future, the shareholders will have one or both of two objectives. One is to achieve a regular and attractive income through the dividends received from the company. The other is to achieve a capital growth in shares where the company becomes successful and therefore its share price on the stock market increases. The owner of the shares can sell these shares at a profit. Of course, companies do not have any specific knowledge on the aims of the shareholders and therefore apply a general approach. The details of this approach are set out in accounting standards which we discuss later.

Employees and Their Unions

Generally, these possible users wish to assess the security of their jobs, employment opportunities, and the security of their pensions. From the unions' position, they will be attempting to negotiate pay increases and other benefits for their members. Knowledge of the financial status of the company will be invaluable in these negotiations as the trade union wishes to evaluate the company's "ability to pay." Individual employees may be interested in their career prospects and security of employment within the company. Obviously, the future looks more attractive to an employee in a financially successful company.

Lenders

They wish to assess whether their loans and the interest will be paid. If the loan is short term, it is likely the lender is interested in the current cash position of the company and how likely it is to change in the future. Long-term lenders will need information on the future stability of the company and the probability of the interest on the loan being paid and the loan principle being repaid at the end of its term. The long-term lender may also wish to assess the probability of the loan being repaid in full if the company goes bankrupt.

Suppliers and Other Trade Creditors

These are clients, customers, and others who wish to know whether they will be paid and if the entity is likely to be a long-term customer. Some suppliers are particularly dependent on one or two large customers. If those companies go out of business, then the supplier will go out of business. If the customer is expanding, the supplier can feel confident about the future.

In addition to these main users, there may be many others, all with their own information needs.

Customers want to know about the future of the entity, particularly if they have warranties or may require replacement parts or repairs in the future. Governments and their agencies need to regulate and collect tax from business entities and use company information in national planning and for statistics. The public are often affected by the activities of large entities, whether it is the donations the entities make to charities, the training they offer, their involvement with community activities, or the pollution they cause.

In recent years, with the increasing globalization of accounting standards, there have been some suggestions on revising the Conceptual Framework. The argument being put forward is that the primary users of financial statements are the providers of capital and that the information should be directed toward their needs which are decision making on their investments. Other groups are considered to be secondary users and should find benefits from the information made public, but it is not particularly prepared for them. However, as we will discuss in Chapter 5, interest is no longer directed only at the financial activities of a company but on such issues as its impact on the environment.

Reporting Financial Transactions

The process of recording and reporting financial transactions slowly developed. Forms of regulation were implemented to ensure that organizations produced certain financial information on their activities. Such regulation may have been legally required, and the rules and regulations containing legislative and non-legislative pronouncements governing financial accounting and reporting became more sophisticated. These regulatory requirements usually were referred to as accounting standards. Undoubtedly, in all countries, accountants would have been closely involved in the development of accounting standards but demands and pressures of national political and economic environments largely formed the way that countries established their own standard setting body. The structure, operation, and authority of the national standard setters were established within a country's current legal system, the types of businesses, and the beliefs and culture within that country.

In all countries, accounting standard setters worked within a coalition of interests including reporting organizations, shareholders, the media, political groups, religious and social values, and others. The powers of these interested parties differed, and the need and desire of the accounting standard setters to gain the support of particular factions also varied. The result was that individual countries set their own accounting standards, and this led to some problems.

In the latter half of the 20th century, there were some highly publicized examples of very profitable companies in Europe that wanted to list shares on the New York Stock Exchange (NYSE). To do so, the profitable company had to redraft its financial information to comply with the U.S. accounting standards, known as Generally Accepted Accounting Standards (GAAP). The result sometimes was that the previously declared profit for a company calculated according to its own accounting standards became a loss when redrafted to comply with the U.S. GAAP as required for a listing on the NYSE. We had arrived at the unhappy position where accounting for financial recording and reporting differed depending on the country in which the company was operating.

A well-publicized case was that of Daimler Benz AG, a German company wishing to list its shares on the U.S. Stock Exchange in the early 1990s. To do so, it had to reconcile the profit it had shown for 1993 using German accounting standards with what the profit would have been if it had used the U.S. GAAP. The net income, or profit, the company had reported in its German financial statements was a healthy DM615 million. After the company had made all the adjustments to comply with the U.S. GAAP, the reported net income turned to a net loss of DM1,839 million. To say that Daimler Benz either made a good profit or a substantial loss depending on which country's regulations were applied was unacceptable. One might even say laughable, and it did not reflect well on the accounting discipline.

This problem of the appropriate treatment of accounting recording being country specific had been recognized earlier. In 1973, national accountancy bodies from Australia, Canada, France, Germany, Mexico, the Netherlands, the United Kingdom and Ireland, and the United States established the International Accounting Standards Committee (IASC). These countries agreed that the IASC would formulate and publish, in the public interest, accounting standards to be observed in the presentation of financial statements and to promote their worldwide acceptance and observance. This would be achieved by ensuring that published financial statements issued by companies complied with IASs in all material respect. It only needed to persuade governments, national standard setting bodies, authorities controlling securities markets and the industrial and business community that published financial statements should comply with IASs. A daunting task!

There were a number of factors assisting the IASC in achieving its aims. Many emerging economies were attempting to establish themselves in international trade or to move away from command economies. There was encouragement also from several organizations and countries wishing to pursue the goal of international harmonization more rapidly and effectively.

These developments encouraged the IASC to adopt a more proactive approach. It refined its earlier objectives and defined its role as:

- Developing robust standards to satisfy the needs of international capital markets and the international business community
- Producing and helping to implement accounting standards that satisfy financial reporting needs of developing and newly industrialized nations
- Achieving greater compatibility between national accounting requirements and IASs

In 1995, the IASC embarked on an ambitious program to issue a set of core standards. This was completed in 1999 with 15 new or revised standards, which reduced the number of alternative methods available to companies and established benchmark treatments and permitted variations. Although the IASC was successful in the core standards project, in retrospect, it is easy to see that the work it was attempting to undertake was impossible due to the way the organization was structured and resourced. It did not have the resources for establishing firm regulations for worldwide accounting and having the power to enforce them. The only way forward was to establish a more powerful and better funded organization and the IASB was established formally in April 2001, but it took many years to arrive at that point. We discuss the successes and the failures of the IASB in Chapter 2.

Measuring Financial Transactions

To complete this section on recording and reporting financial transactions, we need to discuss the very debatable subject on the way we should measure financial transactions and there are various methods. In this section, we explain the main methods, starting with the one that is currently used, but subsequently discussing other methods, some of which may appear more useful than the one currently applied.

Historical Cost

Traditionally, this has been the approach favored by accountants. Using this method, assets are recorded at the amount paid for them at the time of their acquisition. Liabilities are recorded at the amount of proceeds received in exchange for the obligations or the amount of cash to be paid to satisfy the liability in the normal course of business.

The great advantage of historical cost is its reliability. You know exactly how much was paid for the asset and there will in all probability be a paper trail that can be used to verify the cost. You know how much you have to pay to settle any liability you have incurred.

The disadvantage of the historical cost approach is the poor input that the information gives to users for decision making, particularly after the passage of time. Companies may have acquired premises, land, and machinery over the years. If they were recorded at historical cost, they will remain in the records at that amount. After several years, because of changes in prices, the values the assets are shown at will be out of date. Some companies still have properties in their accounts that were purchased over 100 years ago and this original cost is maintained by most companies.

Current Cost

This is sometimes referred to as replacement value or current entry value. For assets, it is the amount that would have to be paid if the same or similar asset was acquired currently, in other words how much it would cost to replace that asset. Liabilities are valued at the amount of cash that would be needed to settle the liability.

Realizable Value

This is sometimes known as current exit value. Assets are shown at the amount that could be obtained if the asset were sold in an orderly disposal, that is, not in a bankruptcy. Liabilities are valued at the amount of cash that would be needed to settle the liability.

Present Value

This is sometimes known as value in use. Assets are shown in the balance sheet at the discounted value of the future cash flows that the asset is expected to generate in the normal course of business. Liabilities are carried at the present discounted net value of the future cash flows expected to be required to settle the liabilities in the normal course of business.

We will use an introductory example to demonstrate how these concepts might be applied.

Example

Company A needs a loan but the only asset it has is a machine that is used in production. The company knows that the bank manager will want to use the machinery for security and will ask its value. The company has managed to obtain the following information.

Historical Cost.   The machine costs $250,000 five years ago and is expected to continue to produce for a further five years. The machine will have no scrap value at the end of that time.

Current Cost.   As prices have increased over the last five years, it would cost $300,000 to replace the machine. This would be basically the same model.

Realizable Value.   As industry is booming and the machine has been well maintained, the company is confident that it could sell the machine for $175,000.

Present Value.   The company believes that, after deducting all costs of running the machine, it will receive $100,000 in cash each year for the next five years from the output it will sell.

The problem is to decide what the value of the machine is. If we use historical cost, we have the reliable purchase cost of $250,000, but the machine is half-way through its useful life. The company will depreciate the machine annually so the amount shown in the company's accounts is likely to be $125,000. They will have written off half of the cost of the machine over the last five years and will write off the remaining half over the next five years. But the amount of $125,000 is not intended to show the "value" of the machine, but is an indication of the proportion of the original cost that has been already written off in the financial statements.

The current cost is the value of a new machine but the machine the company owns is five years old. We could arrive at a calculated, but arbitrary, value by taking just half of the value of the new machine to represent the age of the old machine. This gives a value of $150,000. Do we really, or more importantly the bank, believe this is the current value?

The realizable value of $175,000 looks a useful guide to the value. Of course, there are often many circumstances where the company is unable to sell the machine. Also, how confident are we that there are likely purchasers willing to complete the transactions? This also poses the question as to why does the company not sell the machine as it would receive $25,000 more than the amount it has in its books. The answer to that is in the final method of measurement.

By keeping the machine and continuing to sell the output, the company will receive a cash surplus of $100,000 for the next five years. It is obviously better for the company to keep the machine rather than to sell it. There is one refinement that we need to make to this amount and that is the calculation of the present value of the future cash flows known as "discounting." This involves calculating the current value of future cash flows.

Identifying Financial Information

The Search for Concepts

The perceived need for accounting concepts is not a recent concern but has been evident for many years. An article by Badua (2019) entitled as "Lies, Sex, and Suicide: Teaching Fundamental Accounting Concepts With Sordid Tales From the Seamier Side of Accounting History" identifies the need for identifying concepts. However, reaching agreement on what those concepts are and how they should be applied in recording accounting transactions has not been easy.

Certain assumptions or concepts have been developed to define and categorize which financial transactions and events should be recorded and how. Over the years, it has been found necessary to formalize these concepts so that accountants use the same basis in preparing financial statements and the users of those statements can better understand the information that is being communicated. There are many concepts which are also referred to as assumptions, conventions, principles, and axioms. Some of these concepts are known as "qualitative characteristics." This means the attributes that information should have in order to make it a valuable communication. For example, you would not expect the information to be biased or so incomplete that you might misinterpret it.

There have been differences between the approaches to the task by the FASB in the United States and the IASB. The divergent views have been well explained by Whittington (2008) who argued that there were two world views on the Conceptual Framework. These were a Fair Value View, implicit in the IASB's public pronouncements, and an Alternative View implicit in publicly expressed criticisms of the IASB's pronouncements. These opposing views have continued. The IASB issued in March 2018 a Conceptual Framework for Financial Reporting and the FASB has issued several papers on the topic.

Given the differences between the two main accounting standard setters and the conflicting opinions and changes of view over time by anyone involved in the subject, we hesitate to attempt to offer a firm and comprehensive guide to accounting concepts. Therefore, we list below some of the main concepts, but offer the advice that this list could be lengthened and changed depending on the literature you read.

Business entity concept, which views the business as separate from its owner as far as the financial transactions are concerned.

Going concern assumes that the financial statements are prepared for an organization that is going to continue in business and is not going to close in the foreseeable future.

Matching concept, which accounts for the expenses it has incurred in a financial period and matches them with the revenue generated in that same period.

Consistency, which requires the same accounting treatment to be used from one accounting period to the next unless there is a very good reason to change.

Money measurement, which assumes that only the items that are capable of being measured reliably in financial terms are included in the financial records.

Historical cost, which values assets on their original cost, which is when the transaction or event originally took place. No adjustments are made for subsequent changes in price or value.

We would emphasize that these are some of the concepts that underpin the recording and reporting of financial transactions. To understand the financial reports by any organization, it is necessary to be familiar with the concepts that have influenced the construction of the financial statements. It is also necessary to know if the standard setters, no matter in which country they reside, have adopted a principles- or rules-based approach, which we explain in the following section.

Underlying Assumptions

In addition to the above concepts or assumptions, there are two concepts that are fundamental to accounting: the accruals concept and the going concern concept. These are so important that the IASB has included them in a pronouncement entitled "Framework for the Preparation and Presentation of Financial Statements." This is an old document, also known as the Conceptual Framework, published in 1989 and there are proposals for bringing it up to date, and a revised IAS, issued in 2003, has made some amendments. Further important changes are expected.

In this section, we will refer to the Conceptual Framework as this is the most comprehensive document. You can think of the Conceptual Framework as a type of theory applied to financial statements. It includes two parts which are specifically concerned with concepts or assumptions. One deals with *underlying assumptions*, which is referred to as the accruals and going concern assumptions. The other part covers "qualitative characteristics" and there is some overlap with the assumptions we have discussed above.

It is important to remember that the Conceptual Framework is not a standard. It is the basis on which standard setters develop their pronouncements. If a company enters into a transaction or there is an event where no standard exists, the company can refer to the Conceptual Framework for guidance. Some critics may argue that this would provide information but no clarity.

The Accruals Assumption

The IASB states that financial statements must be prepared on the accruals basis. It explains that transactions and other events are recognized as they occur and not when cash or any other consideration such as checks are given or received. These transactions and events must be recorded in the accounting records when they occur and not when any payment is made or received.

In some instances, the transaction and payment may take place at the same time. You go and have your haircut and you pay for it immediately. You may decide to buy a car in 2021 and the dealer allows you one-year interest-free credit. Using the accruals basis, the dealer must record in the business accounts for 2021 the sale of the car although the cash will not be received until 2022.

We can use a nonbusiness personal example to demonstrate the impact of this concept. Assume that you purchased a surf board for $800. A friend of yours is very keen to buy it and offers you $900. You agree to sell the board on June 1 and that is when your friend takes the board but he claims that he cannot pay you until September. Under the accruals basis, the sale takes place on June 1 and, if you were keeping accounting records, that is when you would record it. Unfortunately, you are now $900 poorer from a cash point of view. That is a problem, but it is a cash problem and you must resolve that by ensuring that you collect the money on the agreed date.

The Going Concern Assumption

Financial statements are usually prepared using the assumption that the business is a going concern and will remain so into the foreseeable future. It is assumed that the business does not intend to or need to close down: it is going to continue trading. If there is evidence that this is not the case, for example, the company may have so much debt that it has to close, then the accounts will be drawn up on a different basis. This will often entail looking at the "break-up" value of the business, which is likely to be much less than its value if it were a going concern and shown as such in the financial statements.

Qualitative Characteristics

In addition to these fundamental assumptions, the Framework for the Preparation and Presentation of financial statements refers to the qualitative characteristics of information. These are the attributes that make the information in financial statements useful.

Understandability

The recipients of financial information must be able to understand it fully if the information is to be useful. As we are providing complex financial information, it is assumed that the recipients have a reasonable knowledge of business, economic, and accounting activities and that they are willing to study the information carefully. It is claimed that some accounting standards are so complex that even qualified accountants have difficulty in understanding them. The reality is that some business activities can be extremely complicated and therefore the standards regulating these activities are also complex.

Relevance

Information must be relevant to the needs of the potential users and should assist users in making a decision. To achieve relevance of financial information, the needs of the users must be known as well as an understanding of the decisions they wish to make. Of course, there can be many different types of users and one set of financial statements may not be useful to all of them.

Materiality

The financial information must be relevant to the needs of the users. If it assists in the decision making of the user, the information is material. Information is relevant if the possible omission or misstatement of it detracts from the decision making of the user.

Reliability

Information is reliable when there are no material errors or biases. Complete reliability is not possible as financial statements contain assumptions, concepts, and estimates.

Faithful Representation

Financial information must represent what it claims to represent, but it is acknowledged that identifying and accurately measuring some transactions is not always possible.

Substance Over Form

Organizations may enter into formal transactions and agreements that may be misleadingly described or interpreted. Financial statements should be prepared on the economic reality of the transaction and not the legal form.

Neutrality

Financial statements should be free from bias and information should not be purposely selected or presented in such a way as to mislead the user.

Prudence

Caution should be used where it is necessary to make judgments about transactions and events that are uncertain. If all the relevant information is not available, reasonable estimates should be made.

Completeness

A large business will undertake millions of activities in a financial period. Although there should be an intention to achieve completeness, financial statements are summaries shaped by the boundaries of materiality and cost.

Comparability

For users of financial information to be able to compare information from different periods and sources, it must be identified, measured, and disclosed by using comparable methods

Principles Versus Rules

The organizations for setting standards, whether using an international, a U.S., or Islamic basis, can use either a principles-based approach or a rules-based approach. The difference between these approaches to setting accounting standards is extremely important but not always clear. The Securities and Exchange Commission in the United States has stated that the distinction between rules-based and principles-based standards is not well defined and is subject to a variety of interpretations (SEC 2003, p. 5). Not everyone would accept that analysis and it is argued that the word "principle" is a general statement that acts as a guide to action. These principles are intended to capture the underlying economic reality of transactions. In contrast, rules-based accounting standards provide a set of rules with detailed guidance, clarifications, and precise answers to questions (Chandra and Azam 2019).

With the principles-based approach, the preparer and auditors of the financial statements have the responsibility to use their judgment and experience to ensure the financial statements give a true and fair view. A rules-based approach assumes that if you follow the rules strictly when preparing financial statements, they will not be misleading. In the subsequent chapters where we discuss the approaches of different accounting standard setters, we will focus on the importance of these two very different approaches in setting standards. In this section, we provide explanations of the terms and their possible effect on financial accounting.

The argument against adhering strictly to the rules is that it excludes professional judgment resulting in decisions that are consistent with the rules but inconsistent with the principle of providing the most useful financial information to users. There is also the danger that the preparers of financial statements may comply with the rules, and are beyond criticism, but may stretch the limits of what is permissible under the law, even though it may not be ethically or morally acceptable or even good accounting. Conversely, it can be argued that the principles-based approach gives too much scope to preparers and auditors for creative accounting. Also, without strict rules to be followed, individual companies will choose different accounting treatments and the characteristic of comparability will be lost. Most of the literature in this area has a tendency to favor the principles-based approach to accounting. An experimental study by Cohne, Krishnamoorthy, Peytcheva, and Wright (2013) concluded that auditors are more likely to constrain aggressive reporting under principles-based accounting standards than under rules-based accounting standards in both stronger and weaker regulatory regimes.

The IASB had always been adamant that it uses a "principles-based approach" to develop its standards. This is not just a small matter of terminology but goes to the philosophy underpinning the nature of standards. The thinking of the IASB may have been shaped by the long-held tenet in the United Kingdom that financial statements should give a "true and fair view." The concept of true and fair view first appeared in the United Kingdom in the Joint Stock Companies Registration and Regulation Act of 1844 (McGregor 1992). Over the years, there has been debate over its meaning and, in 1983, the Accounting Standards Committee in the United Kingdom took counsel's opinion. The advice was that in the end the decision would be made by a judge but courts would consider compliance with accounting principles as prima facie evidence that the accounts are true and fair (Hoffman and Arden 1983). The implication of this advice is that the obligation to give a true and fair view takes precedence over all other accounting requirements of company legislation and accounting standards.

Although our discussion in this section of the issues may appear to be merely academic arguments, the hurdle that has delayed the adoption of international accounting by all countries is the differences between a principles-based approach and a rules-based approach. In subsequent chapters, we explain the drivers that lead to the type of accounting that a company uses and the implications. Although IAS 1 used the term "financial presentation," the ability to "override" the requirements of accounting standards was maintained, even though some argued that its interpretation was very different from true and fair. Evans (2003) critically examined the evidence and concluded that the override in IAS 1 should be viewed in its narrowest possible interpretation and not as an independent all-pervasive fundamental concept. A different and more philosophical stance was taken by Alexander and Jermakowicz (2006). They contended that the "underlying economics of any company," as a reality, cannot exist independently of a conceptual scheme agreed between "human actors." Subsequent articles by other authors have also made suggestions and counterclaims. On a more practical basis, it is argued that "the 'true and fair view' is not easy as ever-evolving regulation and changes in accounting standards mean that the 'true and fair' goalposts keep moving" (O'Keefe and Hackett 2012).

Given the above background, it is not surprising that the debate on the principles/rules approach is so heated and explains the problems that some countries have in adopting International Financial Reporting Standards completely. It is not just a case of exchanging one set of regulations for another. National regulators differ in their authority, size of budget, thoroughness of process, and competence of staff, and the "regulatory culture" differs from country to country. Additionally, some countries prefer a principles-based approach to regulations; others are more comfortable with a rules-based approach.

Determining whether a country adopts a rules-based approach or a principles-based approach is subject to debate. Generally, it could be argued that countries following international standards follow a principles-based approach. Those countries adopting U.S. standards use a rules-based approach. We would emphasize that this "could be argued" and others may reject that conclusion.

For Islamic accounting, the standards were developed considering that, in most cases, Islamic institutions encounter accounting problems due to existing accounting standards such as IFRSs or local GAAP being developed based on conventional institutions and conventional product structures or practices and may be perceived to be insufficient to account for and report Islamic financial transactions. It ought to be mentioned in this respect that, even within the Muslim world, there is disagreement on which accounting standards to follow. In Malaysia, for example, the Malaysian Accounting Standard Board argues that the financial reporting principles in the IFRS do not conflict with Islamic laws (Sharia). Such views are not shared by other Muslim countries (i.e., Saudi Arabia). Islamic accounting will be explained later in Chapter 4.

Legal and Political Issues

As countries have different approaches to the regulation of businesses, we confine our comments to those companies that have some form of legal liability and, in all probability, are listed on a stock exchange. Governments want successful businesses because they provide goods and services and also employment. Possibly, more importantly, they also provide a substantial contribution in tax to the government. Understandably, governments wish to retain control of activities within their sphere and this includes financial reporting activities. Although there are independent boards that determine accounting standards, it is the government that has substantial authority on the disclosure of information by companies and the general conduct of companies such as what they are permitted to do, in which countries they can operate, the safety of their products, and other factors that are legalized.

One issue confronting regulators is that companies may take actions to lessen the amount of tax they are obliged to pay. If there are tax reforms in a country, it can affect economic performance by changing incentives for business formation, expansion, and operation. There are several examples of companies moving profits to lower tax countries. Multinational corporations have opportunities, and face competitive pressures, to shift profits from high corporate tax rate countries to low corporate tax rate countries.

It is argued (Auerbach, Devereux, Keen, and Vella 2017) that there are three common ways of shifting taxable profits between countries: through manipulation of transfer prices, the use of debt, and locating intangible assets in low taxed jurisdictions. The collection of tax from organizations is one of the main methods by which governments are able to address poverty and inequality in their own country. It is suggested that big businesses have the ability to avoid or reduce tax in a country thus depriving governments across the globe of the finance they need to address poverty and invest in health care, education, and jobs.

The Joker in the Pack—Inflation

Unfortunately, using money as a measure of company performance can be unhelpful because of inflation. Some would even argue that it makes no sense as the information, over years, is useless for comparative purposes. The highest inflation rate in the United States in the last 15 years was 3.8 percent in 2008 and in the United Kingdom 3.86 percent in 2011. In Saudi Arabia, the rate averaged 1.93 percent from 2000 until 2020, reaching a high of 11.10 percent in July 2008 and a record low of −5 percent in December 2018. These are general inflation rates, but different items within a country will show different rates. Fluctuations in inflation impact on the financial statements of companies and mean that drawing any conclusions from financial statements must be taken with great care, particularly if making judgments based on several years of operation.

The impact of inflation leads to misinformation for the user of financial statements. For example, if you examine a company's balance sheet, most fixed assets will be shown at their original cost less the cumulative depreciation. If the assets were purchased at different times, the money measurement of cost may be different. Machinery purchased on one date with a life of 10 years may be replaced at the end of that period with similar machinery but the cost is likely to be higher. The amounts in the financial statements do not reflect the "value" of machinery at any one particular moment. In fact, the depreciated value depends on the method of depreciation used by a company. The FASB has emphasized that depreciation is a process of allocation of cost over the period an asset is used and not valuation of the asset at any particular date.

The discussion on whether inflation should be recognized in financial statements is not a recent phenomenon. In March 1976, the Securities and Exchange Commission issued a new disclosure rule requiring all large American nonfinancial corporations to include in their 1976 10-Ks supplementary information on the replacement cost of fixed assets and inventory, as well as income statement charges for depreciation and cost of sales based on those numbers. The SEC was attempting to resolve the concern about the effect of inflation on the numbers appearing in historical cost financial statements.

The United Kingdom attempted to resolve accounting for inflation problem in the 1980s with the Sandilands Report (1996). This attempt has been analyzed by Robson (1994) who puts forward the proposition that "From the perspective of an economist one might say that inflation accounting becomes a problem because inflation is a problem." Certainly there was a lack of enthusiasm with Sandilands suggestions. To many commentators, there were three basic issues: first, the unit of measurement; second, the basis for measuring costs; and third, the concept of profit and loss. The general conclusion was that the Sandilands proposals contain serious theoretical and practical difficulties.

Standard setters were very aware that inflation had a major impact on the value of financial statements, if they were only showing historical costs. The FASB in the United States finally adopted inflation accounting in the form of its Statement No. 33 on Financial Reporting and Changing Prices, which required supplemental financial statements in 1979 annual reports. A total of 1,200 to 1,300 U.S. publicly owned companies were required to disclose both constant dollar and current cost data in addition to their primary, historical cost financial statements. In the United Kingdom, the Accounting Standards Committee issued Statement of Standard Accounting Practice SSAP 16. In both countries, the regulations were withdrawn after a few years. This withdrawal may have been due to the perceived inadequacies of the standard and the difficulties experienced by companies, accountants, and investors in understanding them. Another factor, if we can suggest it, may have been the decline in the rate of depreciation at that time.

Conclusions

The recording and reporting of financial transactions conducted by businesses is extremely important and the information generated is used by many individuals, groups, and governmental organizations in all countries. Given the importance of the financial information, questions arise as to the value of such information. We have pointed out the issues surrounding the use of historical cost as a measure of activity and explained the concepts, and one may even use the word assumptions, in reporting and recording financial information.

This brings us to the major question of why business organizations in different countries do not use the same methods for recording and reporting financial transactions. We accept that in international trade different currencies will be used and we know that there is immediate information on changes in exchange rates. But the countries may have very different ways of "accounting" for transactions so a comparison of financial statements on a worldwide basis can be impossible unless there is some agreement on the measurement methods.

Governments do not set accounting standards, although they rely on them heavily for the regulation of companies and, in some countries,

have substantial influence on their contents. After many decades of countries deciding their own accounting regulations, we have now moved,
very hesitantly, to a partial understanding (we do not use the word agreement) with three major approaches for setting standards. We discuss these
approaches in the following chapters. We focus on the requirements for
the larger companies and the shares in these will be most likely quoted
on a stock exchange. The three major methods for regulating financial
accounting described in the following chapters are:

Chapter 2 IASB with its main base being in the United Kingdom
Chapter 3 FASB based in the United States
Chapter 4 Islamic accounting

To prevent any excitement on the part of readers who may conclude
we are almost there, we would conclude this chapter by mentioning that
many countries individually set their own accounting standards and we
do not know the quality of those standards. Perhaps, more importantly,
we continue to use money as our measure despite its "flexibility." We have
no solution to that problem but, in Chapter 5, "The Future of Corporate
Reporting," we discuss the stage we have reached and what the future
may hold.

CHAPTER 2

International Accounting

Introduction

At one time, there were no accounting standards that required company compliance. Companies decided which methods and processes they used to account for their activities. Many "business-type" activities would be conducted by the owner and sometimes recorded only by memory. For smaller businesses, with only a few owners, this usually caused few problems and the main concern was agreeing a figure with the tax authorities, if this was needed or regarded as necessary. As time passed, businesses grew bigger, and shareholders and lenders entered into the procedures. The approach to compiling financial information was still the responsibility of the owner, but relying on this type of financial information could "scarcely avoid arriving at erroneous conclusions" (Naylor 1960). To protect those who use the financial statements of companies for investment decisions, many countries began to develop their own accounting standards.

Frequently, it was an organization of professional accountants in a country which instructed its members the methods they should use for recording financial transactions and operational activities. This guidance was usually focused on the operation of local businesses, but gradually it was the national, political, and economic environments that formed the accounting standards that were developed in a particular country. Yamey (1994) claims that accounting became increasingly important in the United Kingdom in the 19th century with the rise of the corporate economy and large-scale business enterprise. The structure, operation, and authority of the standard setters were developed within existing practices and conventions of that particular country. In the United States, accounting for the transactions of an entity, rather than for the value of the proprietary interests of the entity's owners, can be traced to the late 19th century (Colson 2005). The accounting standards developed, although applicable within a particular country, have no, or very little, impact on policies and procedures in other countries.

National standard setters worked within a coalition of interests, including reporting organizations, shareholders, media, and political groups. The powers of these interested parties differed, and the need and desire of the accounting standard setters to gain the support of these particular factions also varied. Country-specific standards were helpful in regulating accounting in one country but, as international trade developed, a better approach to measuring and recording financial transactions was required. This led to the development of accounting standards intended to apply internationally.

In this chapter, we commence with the early business developments that demonstrated the need for an international approach to standard setting. This is followed by a review of the development of International Accounting Standards (IASs). Our final section explains the structure and operation of the present International Accounting Standards Board (IASB).

The South Sea Bubble and Daimler Benz

The development of the establishment of international accounting regulations can be traced back many years to around the 18th century. There are two events that can be identified as illustrating the events that took place over many centuries. These two happenings have no direct relationship but are examples of the issues arriving from having no accounting standards, even national ones, or only using accounting standards set at the country level. The first example, well described by Balen (2003), is 300 years old but not only demonstrates the rampant nature of unfettered greed, but also questions the actions of the government in England at that time. The situation involved the government at that time, which had substantial current debts and considered that an offer of exclusive trading rights with Spain's colonies in South America would be an incentive to convince the private sector to assume these debts. Unfortunately, the trading rights were not as extensive as suggested but stories of South

American gold and silver ready to be imported to Europe attracted investors' attention.

Rumors of enjoying substantial wealth by buying stock greatly increased the share price. In January 1720, the "South Seas" share price was £128. Four months later, the price was a spectacular £550. This substantial, but unfortunately totally misleading, increase in the South Seas share price encouraged the growth of other companies offering business proposals that ranged from the doubtful to the totally implausible. The situation had become frantic and, to install some level of control, the English Parliament passed the "Bubble Act" in 1720.

This permitted the legal incorporation of new joint-stock companies for many different business activities, which enabled enthusiastic shareholders to buy different proportions of company stock. This government action resulted in even more joint stock companies being registered and there was a stock market frenzy. Although the South Sea Company was not reporting good profits, by August 1720 the share price was £1,000. Not surprisingly, there was a meltdown.

Speculators who had purchased shares on credit and still held them often became bankrupt. In September, the shares hit a low of £150 and, as the companies were unlimited, the shareholders were personally liable for all of the debts of a company should it fail. The investors were somewhat, one might argue substantially, saddened by these events. Pressure was put on the government to take action and the Bubble Act was repealed in 1825. New legislation was introduced that both limited the amount of liability for shareholders and introduced greater control of company activities. These unfortunate experiences for UK shareholders had the beneficial consequence of introducing greater control of the financial aspects of companies. However, these legal improvements were only at a single country level.

Although a period of setting accounting standards followed the events of the Bubble, this practice developed individually in various countries. Not surprisingly, as we are concerned with events that occurred many years ago, there were significant differences in the accounting regulations in the individual countries. This was accepted as inevitable and few problems of having only national legislation were experienced as international trade was not developed to any extent. That situation was to change dramatically but not immediately.

It was not until the latter half of the 20th century that some very successful and profitable European companies decided it would be advantageous to list shares on the New York Stock Exchange (NYSE). This was a time when each country was still setting its own accounting standards. To list on the NYSE, European companies had to redraft their financial statements in accordance with U.S. GAAP.

The case which hit the headlines was Daimler Benz AG, a German company that desired to list its shares on the U.S. Stock Exchange (Widman 1994). To comply with the NYSE regulations, the company was required to recalculate the profit it had shown for 1993 using German GAAP with what the profit would have been if the company had adopted U.S. GAAP. The net income, or profit, the company had reported in its German financial statements was DM615 million. After the company had made all the adjustments to comply with U.S. GAAP, the reported net income turned to a net loss of DM1,839 million. Not only was this, to put it mildly, disappointing for shareholders, it raised the fundamental question of what is profit and how should it be measured.

It was slightly embarrassing, although true, to admit that the amount of a company's profit depended on which country's regulations were used. The major question was whether a company making a loss in one country can draw up its accounts in another country and make a profit. The answer was a confusing and embarrassing "Yes." The obvious solution was to make accounting regulations international. The problem was how this could be achieved. It was now obvious that if every country accounted for transactions in a similar way, there would be no problems. Understandably, one country would not wish to be compelled to use the accounting regulations of another country. One reason could be that the country's government does not wish to cede its authority to another country. A more practical issue is that countries can be very different in the way business is conducted within its own territorial borders. Businesses internationally were different, and a country's regulations were designed to incorporate these features. In the next section, we consider these differences.

International Differences

At an everyday level, we are aware of differences between countries. Possibly the most audible difference is the use of language. Even in a single country with a shared language, there will be some regional variations. Even for differences in measurement values intercountry, a method of translation has been agreed. A 6-foot-tall person will look the same height even if the measurement is taken in another country using metric measurement. However, if we are considering the regulations to be used when drawing up statements demonstrating a company's financial operations, there are several intercountry differences. Attention must be paid to their influence but this raises difficulties which we discuss here.

Legal Systems

There are two main types of legal systems, although there may be some merging of these. At its simplest, there is either a common law system or a code law system. With the common law system, accounting regulations are not part of that system but were usually developed by the country's professional accounting bodies or some other form of independent standard setters without government involvement. With a code law system, there is usually a wide set of rules that give guidance in all situations. Accounting regulations in these systems are often part of the law and controlled by the government either directly or indirectly. The issue is not concerned with developing one accounting system but substantial changes in the legal system.

Tax Systems

Companies, as with individuals, wish to minimize the amount of tax they pay without breaking regulations, although some squeezing may be tried. In some countries, the government may have their own tax regulations to determine the amount of tax a company should pay and this may influence the way financial accounts are prepared using accounting standards. In other countries, the tax regulations are completely separate from the accounting regulations and the tax authorities will require companies to make alterations to their financial statements to comply with tax regulations so that the amount of tax payable is correctly calculated legally. Whichever approach a country takes, the result is the same. The tax authorities will determine how the amount of payable tax is calculated and their calculations most likely will differ from any accounting regulations.

Stock Exchanges

There are about 60 major stock exchanges in the world and these are market places for purchasing and selling shares, bonds, and securities. Companies deciding to register on a stock exchange must comply with the regulations in the country in which it is based. These will include the nature of the financial information to be recorded. Many stock exchanges will require that the financial statements comply with the regulations within their own country. If the country has its own financial regulations, these must be followed, but if the country has adopted IASs, then these should be applied. The NYSE requires companies listed with it to follow U.S. regulations, that is, the accounting standards issued by the U.S. FASB. The NYSE changed its rules in 2007 to enable international companies to use IFRS reporting language in their filings.

The Accounting Profession

In some countries, the accounting profession is very strong and involved in all aspects of corporate financial activities. Before the establishment of formal national accounting standard setters, it was normally the accounting profession that issued advice to its members on the acceptable accounting methods for business transactions. A highly developed accounting profession in a country will have a significant influence on the financial accounting regulations in that country. The members will sit on various committees, act as advisers, sponsor research, and publish papers on the perceived correct way of accounting for business activities.

Culture

Culture is regarded as highly influential on the financial accounting and reporting system in a country, but it is difficult to define the direction and power of its influence. Research has classified countries according to cultural differences. A major influence was the theory that there are four dimensions along which cultural values can be analyzed: individualism–collectivism, uncertainty avoidance, power distance (strength of social hierarchy), and masculinity–femininity (task orientation vs. person orientation) (Hofstede 1980). In Chapter 4, we explain the requirements of Islamic accounting.

Regulations

To understand the financial statements of companies, it is essential to know the regulations they are following and the nature of the business. Any regulations that are applied should be stated clearly, usually by independent auditors, in the annual report and accounts. We show below extracts from three different but well-known companies that demonstrate the differences in regulations. We have put in italics the key sentence.

The first example is from the AstraZeneca Annual Report and Form 20-F Information 2020. The following extract from the annual report and accounts explains the company's approach:

> UK-adopted international accounting standards on 31 December 2020, EU-adopted IFRS was brought into UK law and became UK-adopted international accounting standards, with future changes to IFRS being subject to endorsement by the UK Endorsement Board. The Company Financial Statements will transition to UK-*adopted international accounting standards for* financial periods beginning 1 January 2021.

The second example is from the report of PricewaterhouseCoopers (PwC) for Alibaba Group Holding Limited:

> In our opinion, the accompanying consolidated balance sheets and the related consolidated income statements, consolidated statements of comprehensive income, changes in shareholders' equity and cash flows present fairly, in all material respects, the financial position of Alibaba Group Holding Limited and its subsidiaries (collectively, the "Company") at March 31, 2016 and 2017, and the results of their operations and their cash flows for each of the three years in the period ended March 31, 2017 in conformity with *accounting principles generally accepted in the United States of America.*

The third example is from the independent auditors' report of Deloitte Haskins & Sells LLP for Asian Paints Limited:

> In our opinion and to the best of our information and according to the explanations given to us, the aforesaid standalone financial

statements give the information required by the Companies Act 2013 ("the Act") in the manner so required and *give a true and fair view in conformity with the Indian Accounting Standards* prescribed under section 133 of the Act read with the Companies (Indian Accounting Standards) Rules, 2015, as amended ("Ind AS"), and other accounting principles generally accepted in India, of the state of affairs of the Company as at 31st March, 2020, and its profit, total comprehensive income, its cash flows and the changes in equity for the year ended on that date.

The fourth example is from the independent auditors' report of KPMG for Qatar Islamic Bank:

In our opinion, the accompanying consolidated financial statements present fairly, in all material respects, the consolidated financial position of the Group as at 31 December 2020, and its consolidated financial performance and its consolidated cash flows for the year then ended in accordance with the *Financial Accounting Standards (FAS) issued by the Accounting and Auditing Organization for Islamic Financial Institutions (AAOIFI)*.

Although the examples we have selected are from different but recent time periods, they demonstrate effectively that financial statements are drawn up using different regulatory approaches. The consequence is that if you require to explore the financial statements of a particular country for a specific year, you need to know the regulations that were being used at that time. The good news is that companies listed on a stock exchange will explain their approach. For some other companies, you may not have the same confidence in their pronouncements.

International Accounting Emerges

The previous examples from the financial statements of four different countries demonstrate that the annual report and accounts of a company may be determined by the regulations in that country and can best be understood by knowing those specific regulations. Accounting regulations are not the most exciting reading material. To know them for one country is acceptable but if you need to understand them for several countries, it becomes extremely tedious. The obvious solution to this problem is for all countries to use the same accounting language. In this section, we concentrate on international regulations and the processes companies should be following if the international standards have been adopted.

Like many regulatory bodies, international accounting has developed a language of its own. To help clarify the various institutions and their relationships, we list below some of the abbreviations we are using:

> IASC International Accounting Standards Committee. Established in 1973. Replaced by IASB
> IASB International Accounting Standards Board
> EAA European Accounting Association
> EFRAG European Financial Reporting Advisory Group
> IFRS International Financial Reporting Standard
> SMEs Small- and medium-sized entities
> FRC Financial Reporting Council
> IFRIC International Financial Reporting Interpretations Committee
> FASB Financial Accounting Standards Board United States
> AAOIFI Accounting and Auditing Organization for Islamic Financial Institutions

The Early Days

The movement to construct accounting standards on an international basis came from the accounting profession and not from any government. In making this proposal, the accounting profession did not declare any intention to establish regulations that would serve as a basis for calculating the amount of taxation to be paid by companies in different countries. It was to agree on an international level the method for accounting for financial transactions and for financial reporting. It was illogical that the profit or loss a company declared through its business activities depended on the regulations in which the company resided. The failure to have an international basis for accounting brought the discipline into disrepute. It did not make sense to state that the profit a company made depended on the country in which it operated. The intent was to develop a standard form of financial accounting and reporting for all countries.

The move toward an international form of accounting came from the national accountancy bodies of Australia, Canada, France, Germany, Mexico, the Netherlands, the United Kingdom, Ireland, and the United States. In 1973, a meeting of these countries was held and an agreement was reached to form the IASC which would be a private sector, non-governmental organization. It was agreed that the IASC would be based in London, the United Kingdom. The decision to form the IASC was made when several developments supported the initiative. Trade of goods and services in other countries was increasing. To support this activity, a common set of regulations on accounting treatments was required so that companies could relate to each other. Although the European Union had been formed, there were differences in accounting for accounting transactions in the various member countries. The establishment of IASs set, not by any single government, but by an independent body was welcomed. The decision to make London the base was not explained but we could propose several reasons. The London Stock Exchange is an important user of financial statements, the accounting bodies are well established, and geographically it is easily accessible from other places in the world. We would remind the reader that one of the authors comes from the United Kingdom, which may bias our own opinions!

In the beginning, the IASC had limited funding, as there was no government support from any of the EU countries. The credit for the progress the committee made can be mainly awarded to the accounting professions. Given the limited funding, the IASC held meetings only three or four times annually and there was no intention to formulate a system that would meet the taxation requirements of any one country. At the beginning, it was realized that the IASC would not be able to develop a complete batch of new international standards. The aim, therefore, was harmonization of the existing standards, which were currently being used by the various individual countries. Such an approach offered several benefits. Each country would no longer have the costs of developing its own accounting standards and the financial statements issued by one European country would be understandable to interested parties in all European countries. Finally, the development of a common accounting language will increase involvement from several organizations and would assist the development of European trade.

The IASC issued its first IAS, *IAS 1 Disclosure of Accounting Policies,* in January 1975 and in October 1975 issued *IAS 2 Inventories.* It continued steadily to develop and issue accounting standards and it issued 41 standards between 1975 and 2000. These standards and some of the others it issued are still in force as they have been adopted by the organization that developed from the IASC, which is the IASB.

Establishing accounting standards that can be applied in several countries is complex and expensive and requires the knowledge and expertise of individuals and groups working in harmony. Although there were no criticisms of the work conducted by the IASC and the quality of the standards it had issued, there were some issues. Developing standards was a complex task and the IASC had limited funding and relied heavily on the support of national accounting bodies to complete its work. Although the achievements of the IASC were significant, it became apparent that if full international accounting, adopted by many countries, were to become a reality greater funding was required. To achieve this, the IASC needed to be independent of the national accounting standard setting bodies and find a way of increasing its financial support.

The first stage in becoming more international was the meeting of a number of countries, including Canada, the United Kingdom, the United States, Australia, and New Zealand. The objective of the meeting was to agree to a stronger approach to full internationalization. The result of that meeting was the establishment in January 2001of the IASB. This was not merely a change of name as the IASB had increased funding and developed a new structure. The newly formed IASB commenced developing its own standards entitled International Financial Reporting Standards (IFRSs). The European body, although useful and successful in starting the process, had served its purpose and the objective was a full international approach.

The standards issued by the IASC were not discarded and have remained in existence. The first standard issued was IAS 1 Presentation of Financial Statements and the last one IAS 41 Agriculture. The first standard issued by the IASB was IFRS 1 *First-Time Adoption of International Financial Reporting Standards.* This was a clear declaration by the IASB of its intent for involvement of all countries. This was followed by *IFRS 2 Share-Based Payments*. The issue of IFRSs has resulted in a dual naming of standards. There are now the original IASs issued by the IASC still in existence, for example, IAS 2 Inventories, but also the new IFRSs, for example, IFRS 2 Share-Based Payments. In 2019, there were 16 IFRSs and 29 IASs and all of these are applicable.

In addition to the standards, there are also IFRICs issued by the interpretative body of the IASB. This process involving IFRIC addresses newly identified financial reporting issues not specifically covered in IFRS or issues where unsatisfactory or conflicting interpretations have developed, or seem likely to develop. The first pronouncement was IFRIC 1 Changes in Existing Decommissioning, Restoration and Similar Liabilities and the latest at the date of writing this book was IFRIC 23 Uncertainty Over Income Tax Treatments.

This decision of issuing IFRSs in addition to the existing IASs may not have been the best approach, but it appears to have caused few problems. When discussing several standards generally, it is usual to use the phrase "accounting standards." When referring to a specific standard, the correct IAS or IFRS name should be used.

Unfortunately, events happen which sometimes impact on the existing policies of regulators. When the United Kingdom was part of the EU, all the countries jointly agreed to adopt IASs. The process was for the EU to endorse them. Three criteria were used for endorsement and these had to be satisfied before they become binding for EU-based companies. The three criteria were:

A "true and fair view" criterion
A list of qualitative criteria
A "European public good" criterion

A useful case study of the process is given by Bischof and Daske (2016) and there are various studies concerning adoption by individual European countries.

As the United Kingdom has left the EU, this requirement may be changed. The establishment of BREXIT and the United Kingdom's departure from the EU has had several unforeseen consequences. The requirement for UK listed companies to apply IFRS was enshrined in UK law, by cross reference to the European regulations, referring to IFRS as adopted by the EU. On December 31, 2020, the UK Department for Business, Energy and Industrial Strategy declared that companies need to use UK adopted IASs instead of EU-adopted IAS for financial years beginning on or after January 1, 2021. Both sets of standards were the same on January 1, 2021. You can continue to use EU-adopted IAS when preparing your accounts for financial years beginning before January 1, 2021.

The following example from the UK company Tesco PLC's annual report for 2020 demonstrates the disclosure of financial accounting standards while the United Kingdom was part of the EU.

Note 1 Accounting policies, judgements and estimates General information Tesco PLC (the Company) is a public limited company incorporated and domiciled in the United Kingdom (UK) under the Companies Act 2006 (Registration number 445790). The address of the registered office is Tesco House, Shire Park, Kestrel Way, Welwyn Garden City, AL7 1GA, UK. The main activities of the Company and its subsidiaries (together, the Group) are those of retailing and retail banking. Basis of preparation. The consolidated Group financial statements have been prepared in accordance with International Financial Reporting Standards (IFRS) as endorsed by the European Union (EU).

In their annual report for the financial year ending on February 27, 2021—a lengthy document of 220 pages available on their website—the company states:

in accordance with international accounting standards in conformity with the requirements of the Companies Act 2006 and International Financial Reporting Standards adopted pursuant to Regulation (EC) No 1606/2002 as it applies in the European Union. The Group Financial Statements are also prepared in accordance with IFRS as issued by the International Accounting Standards Board. The Directors have also chosen to prepare the Parent Company financial statements in accordance with United Kingdom Generally Accepted Accounting Practice (United Kingdom Accounting Standards and applicable law), including Financial Reporting Standard (FRS) 101 Reduced Disclosure Framework.

Country Practices

Several countries may claim to have adopted IASs but the extent of the adoption can vary. The International Financial Reporting Standards Foundation uses the term jurisdiction and not country to measure the extent of adoption. It claims that 27,000 domestically listed companies on 88 major stock exchanges in the world use IFRS standards and fuller information can be found on their website at www.iasplus.com/en/resources/ifrs-topics/use-of-ifrs-g20.

This claim of adoption should not be regarded as a measure that a jurisdiction requires all companies within its borders to comply with IFRSs. Usually, it is only major companies listed on its national stock exchange that must apply international standards. Medium-size and smaller companies may follow their national regulations for financial reporting or, if there are none, they comply with the *IFRS for SMEs* standard. SME refers to small- and medium-sized enterprises. Although a country may not have adopted international standards, the essence of them may be captured in their own standard setting process as in Norway (Kvaal 2017). The same could be said about the majority of Muslim countries where IFRS is gaining popularity so long as it does not conflict with Islamic laws.

Although a country or jurisdiction may claim that it applies IASs, caution should be exercised when examining the financial statements of companies within that country (Zeff and Nobes 2010). There are also key words that reveal the extent of adoption. Where a country/jurisdiction claims to have

- *Adopted* international standards, it is normal practice that the standards will apply only to certain organizations, usually the large, listed companies.

- *Endorses* international standards, they may maintain their own standard setting process. A specific international standard will be examined and, if it is considered suitable, will form part of national regulations but the country may require further disclosures or make some changes in the requirements.
- *Adapt* international standards, which may mean that they use the international standard as a basis for making adjustments so that it satisfies their own particular needs.

Financial statements are also subject to a country's political, legislative, tax regulations and other pressures. This can result in differences in financial reporting statements. The year ends of companies can also differ, with new accounting standards being applicable on the annual periods beginning on or after January 1. Some may find that a new standard becomes applicable in their financial year. Others, with an earlier year-end date, will not have to comply with the IFRS until the following year's financial statements. In some countries, for example, Australia and the United Kingdom, corporate accounting periods do not necessarily end on December 31. In other countries, that may be the usual year-end date for all companies. In a comparison of India and China, the authors concluded that accounting estimates in India are useful in predicting future earnings and cash flows, but accounting estimates in China are not. They conclude that accounting quality varies with accounting systems and legal enforcement. Accounting standards in China and India are converging to IFRS, but both countries have not fully implemented IFRS (Eng and Vichitsarawong 2017).

The issue of adopting IFRSs in any country places challenges and these have been documented. Krajňák (2020) conducted a questionnaire survey in 2018 among 28 industrial companies in the selected region of the Czech Republic. He concluded that it is more convenient to prepare financial statements only according to the legislation of national accounting standards with the advantage being lower costs. Fuad, Agung, and Puji (2019) examine whether accounting quality is improved after the convergence process of IFRS. They used industrial companies' data from 2008 until 2014, comprising 3,861 firm-years observations, in Indonesia.

The conclusion was that there is no evidence that accounting quality increased following IFRS convergence. China has "converged" with international standards but research by Cheng, Jing, Sanjian, and Zhang (2019) found that the converged standards are perceived negatively by market participants and the A-share firms in the post-2007 period experienced higher information asymmetry (higher bid-ask spread, higher stock return volatility, and higher analyst forecast dispersion).

We would emphasize that a substantial change in the regulation of financial accounting in a country is likely to cause extensive adjustments both in the collection and in the communication of accounting information. We would not wish to overemphasize this and countries may experience different problems depending on their own requirements. However, the move to IASs is going to involve substantial change for some countries and individual companies. However, not all companies will experience such difficulties.

There is the situation where a company may be well established in a particular country but is foreign owned. For example, Shell Canada Limited (French: *Shell Canada Limitée*) is the subsidiary of Anglo-Dutch Royal Dutch Shell. The following extract from the auditors' note in their annual report explains clearly the relationship and the basis for the financial statements:

- give a true and fair view of the state of Shell's and of the Parent Company's affairs as at December 31, 2020 and of Shell's loss and the Parent Company's income for the year then ended;
- have been properly prepared in accordance with International Accounting Standards in conformity with the requirements of the Companies Act 2006 and, as regards the Group financial statements, both International Financial Reporting Standards (IFRS) adopted pursuant to Regulation (EC) No. 1606/2002 as it applies in the European Union (EU) and IFRS as issued by the international Accounting Standards Board (IASB); and
- have been prepared in accordance with the requirements of the Companies Act 2006.

In searching for the financial statements of a company, it is essential to determine the ownership of the company and its relationship with other companies. Cadbury PLC, well known in the United Kingdom for its chocolates, has an auditor's report which states:

In our opinion:

- the financial statements give a true and fair view of the state of the group's and the parent company's affairs as at 31 December 2009 and of the group's profit for the year then ended;
- the financial statements have been properly prepared in accordance with IFRSs as adopted by the European Union; and
- the financial statements have been prepared in accordance with the requirements of the Companies Act 2006.

Interestingly, Cadbury PLC is owned by Mondelez, a U.S. company, which is one of the world's largest snack companies with global net revenues of $26.6 billion and net earnings of $3.6 billion in 2020. Their portfolio includes snack brands such as Cadbury, Milka, and Toblerone chocolate; Oreo, belVita, and LU biscuits; Halls candy; and Trident gum and Tang powdered beverages. They prepare their consolidated financial statements in conformity with U.S. GAAP. This is required by U.S. law to file a form 10-K with the U.S. Securities and Exchange Commission Washington, D.C. 20549 FORM 10-K.

The International Accounting Standards Board

The Process

The IASB is an independent standard setter responsible for IASs and reports to the International Financial Reporting Standards Foundation Trustees. The process in producing a standard is time consuming and provides opportunities for the preparers and users of financial statements to comment at various stages. The development of an IFRS is a public process, with the results of the various stages being on the IFRS website.

Most standards are focused on specific accounting practices, for example, IFRS 13 Fair Value Measurement. They have similar structures and it is made very clear where and when the requirements of a standard apply. The standard details the disclosures that companies should make in their financial statements and it specifies the measurement methods to be applied. The IFRIC gives guidance if there are problems on the application of a standard and publishes IFRIC Interpretations to explain the requirements. IFRICs have the same authority as a financial accounting standard. The Interpretations Committee also gives guidance on financial reporting issues not specifically addressed in IFRSs.

The Language of International Accounting

As with all disciplines, accounting has a language of its own. Some of the terms have been in use for many centuries while others have been developed by the IASC or the IASB. Baker (2017) argues that the standards-setting process has evolved from an early reliance on accounting theory to the present day where standards are now developed based on a Conceptual Framework. In explaining some of the terms, we consider those most frequently used today, but some of these terms may have been in use long before the advent of the IASB.

The purpose of accounting standards is to ensure that financial information is reliable and informative. This will provide financial statements that present fairly the financial position, financial performance, and cash flows of an organization. The first standard, issued in 1975, *was IAS 1 The Presentation of Financial Statements (IASC 1975)*. This standard has been the subject of many amendments.

In December 2014, IAS 1 was amended by Disclosure Initiative (Amendments to IAS 1) as there had been concerns about some of the existing presentation and disclosure requirements in the standard. In October 2018, the Definition of Material (Amendments to IAS 1 and IAS 8) was issued and, in January 2020, Classification of Liabilities as Current or Non-current was issued. This clarified a criterion in IAS 1 for classifying a liability as noncurrent: the requirement for an entity to have the right to defer settlement of the liability for at least 12 months after the reporting period. This was followed in July 2020 by the Classification of

Liabilities as Current or Non-current—Deferral of Effective Date, which deferred the mandatory effective date of amendments to IAS 1. There is also an extensive list of minor consequential amendments to IAS 1 that have been made over the years. The total standards that have been issued and are mostly still in force are 41 IASs, the last one being IAS 41 Agriculture issued in 2001 and 17 IFRSs. The most recent standard issued at the time of writing this book was IFRS 17 Insurance Contracts issued in 2017.

The requirements of individual standards may be updated over the years. The standard can be revised if there are changes in business practices, or deficiencies or weaknesses are identified in the requirements of the standard. In such cases, the IASB will issue an amendment to the existing standard. Alternatively, the existing standard may be withdrawn and replaced with a new standard. In this case, the new standard usually would have a new number. An update of the possible future changes that may be made to some standards can be found on www.ifrs.org/projects/.

Structure of a Standard

Individual standards have a similar structure and the example we describe below is *IAS 2 Inventories* (IASB 2003). The standard was issued first under that title in 2003 to be effective from 2005. There was an earlier version in 1975 but the latest standard sets out in detail the information to be disclosed by companies.

The standard requires inventories to be measured at lower cost and net realizable value (NRV) and outlines methods for determining cost. NRV is the amount that can be gained upon the sale or other disposal of an asset, less an estimate of the costs involved. Inventories include assets held for sale in the ordinary course of business (finished goods), assets in the production process for sale in the ordinary course of business (work in process), and materials and supplies that are consumed in production (raw materials).

IAS 2 excludes certain inventories from its scope, examples being:

- Work in process arising under construction contracts
- Financial instruments

- Biological assets related to agricultural activity and agricultural produce at the point of harvest

The main sections of the standard are given here.

Objectives

A standard cannot be understood properly without an appreciation of what it is trying to accomplish. In the case of IAS 2, it is to set out as the accounting treatment for inventories. It identifies what the problem is and explains how the standard addresses it.

Scope

This explains what transactions and events are covered by the standard and which are excluded. IAS 2, for example, applies to all inventories except work in progress in construction contracts, financial instruments, and biological assets. Exclusions usually arise because they are dealt with in another standard.

Definitions

The key terms used in the standard are defined. This is extremely important as some standards are very technical, and the definitions assist in the correct application of the standards.

Measurement of Inventories

In many standards, measurement is the longest section. IAS 2 states that the cost of inventories comprises all costs of purchase, costs of conversion, and other costs incurred in bringing the inventories to their present condition. There follow several subsections explaining what is meant by these terms and how the measurement takes place. For example, a company may purchase cloth, convert this into men's shirts, wrap them in attractive paper, and send to their stores to be sold.

Recognition as an Expense

It is essential that a company knows when to deal with inventories as an expense, as this will determine the profit for the financial period.

Disclosures

The standard very carefully lists all the information that must be disclosed by an entity in its financial statements. With inventories, the list is fairly short, starting with the disclosure of "accounting policies used in measuring inventories" and ending with "the carrying amount of inventories pledged as securities." Some standards are primarily concerned with the appropriate disclosure of information and will contain a lengthy list of requirements.

Effective Date

It is essential for entities to know when they must start complying with the standard. Usually, the IASB permits at least 12 months to allow companies to adopt their accounting records and procedures so that the information can be captured. It is also normal for the standard to encourage entities to adopt the standard early if they so desire.

Appendices

In the appendices, there is a basis for conclusions explaining the reasons for the IASB's requirements. With some standards, there may be several examples of how the standard should be applied in different circumstances.

Standards have paragraphs in bold type and in plain type. These paragraphs have equal authority. The paragraphs in bold type indicate the main principles but they do not have greater authority than other paragraphs.

The Main Financial Statements

In September 2007, the IASB identified the financial statements that a company should provide in its annual report and accounts. These statements were explained in *IAS 1 Presentation of Financial Statements* (IASB 2007) as follows:

- A statement of financial position as at the end of the period;
- A statement of profit and loss and other comprehensive income for the period. Other comprehensive income is those items of income and expense that are not recognized in profit or loss in accordance with IFRS standards. IAS 1 allows an entity to present a single combined statement of profit and loss and other comprehensive income or two separate statements;
- A statement of changes in equity for the period;
- A statement of cash flows for the period;
- Notes, comprising a summary of significant accounting policies and other explanatory information; and
- A statement of financial position as at the beginning of the preceding comparative period when an entity applies an accounting policy retrospectively or makes a retrospective restatement of items in its financial statements, or when it reclassifies items in its financial statements.

Companies are not required to use these terms but may choose to do so. In our experience, many companies do not use the term statement of financial position but the term balance sheet. Also, the use of only one statement entitled statement of profit or loss account and other comprehensive income is not frequently adopted. The information is provided in two separate statements, one entitled either the profit or loss account or the income statement and the other statement of comprehensive income.

The standard requires that the financial statements should contain comparative information in respect of the preceding period. There are also extensive notes to the accounts that explain the policies and procedures the company has followed in constructing their main financial statements. These notes can require several pages. One criticism of the

notes is that some companies merely copy the most important requirements of a standard without explaining its importance to its own financial performance.

In identifying the main financial statements, there are separate standards that explain the information required in that statement. As an
example of the application of standards, we restrict our observations on
the separate standards that are concerned with the specific contents of the
statement of financial position.

The Balance Sheet (Statement of Financial Position)

Needless to say, the balance sheet will always balance and the value given
to all the assets will equal the amount that the company has borrowed
plus the investments made by the shareholders. This relationship is usually clarified by what is known as the accounting equation. The basis of
the equation is that a company does not have any wealth of its own. To
acquire assets, such as buildings and machinery, it will require funding.
This comes from shareholders and is known as equity or capital. In addition, the company may borrow money from a bank or other sources to
purchase assets and this borrowing establishes the company's liabilities.
The relationship between the assets, capital, and other liabilities in the
business forms the *accounting equation* which is:

Assets = Capital + Liabilities

The above three items can be expanded to represent:

**Noncurrent assets + current assets = Capital and reserves +
long-term liabilities + current liabilities**

This sequence can be reordered and, instead of adding current liabilities to the right-hand side of the equation, it can be deducted from the
left-hand side. The accounting equation still balances. We show below a
simple example similar to the structure used by most companies:

Example balance sheet

	$	$
Non-current assets		500
Current assets	300	
Less current liabilities	200	100
		600
Loans	150	
Shareholders' equity	450	600

There are some specific requirements in the standard. Assets must be identified as either current assets or noncurrent assets and shown separately. Although the standard does not give a specific definition of noncurrent assets, it does give one for current assets. If an asset does not come under this definition, it must be a noncurrent asset. Cash held by the company is a current asset. Also, a payment expected to be received 12 months of the date of the balance sheet is regarded as a current asset.

Other examples of current assets are those items expected to be sold or used within the company's normal operating cycle or held for the purposes of trading. For example, a retailer will have goods for sale and a manufacturer will hold raw materials as part of its production cycle. These fall under the classification of inventories.

The standard defines what is meant by current liabilities with other liabilities being noncurrent. Essentially, these are amounts the company owes and are expected to be paid within 12 months of the company's current balance sheet date. Noncurrent assets are usually much greater in value than those of current assets.

Although the standard explains the information that should be included on a statement of financial position, each of the items requires its own standards. The following list are those standards that may be relevant to a particular company's balance sheet specific to the contents of the statement of financial position:

IAS 16—Property Plant and Equipment
IAS 23—Borrowing Costs
IAS 38—Intangible Assets
IAS 36—Impairment of Assets

IAS 38—Intangible Assets

IAS 39—Financial Instruments

IAS 40—Financial Instruments

IFRS 5—Non-current Assets Held for Sale and Discontinued Operations

IFRS 7—Financial Instruments: Disclosures

IFRS 9—Financial Instruments

Of course, the items shown on the face of the statement of financial position will depend on the size and nature of the company. Here, we show the main headings from the balance sheet for 2020 for a large UK company, Rio Tinto:

Noncurrent assets Goodwill

Intangible assets

Property, plant, and equipment

Investments in equity accounted units

Inventories

Deferred tax assets

Receivables and other assets

Tax recoverable

Other financial assets

Current assets

Inventories

Receivables and other assets

Tax recoverable

Other financial assets

Cash and cash equivalents

The IASB Work Plan

The IASB has a very comprehensive website and it regularly issues information on the various projects on which it is currently working or has completed. As a guide to the substantial amount of information that is easily available, we show here the key details of the work plan that was issued in February 2021:

Standard setting projects

Management Commentary

Maintenance projects

Accounting Policies and Accounting Estimates —

Disclosure Initiative — Accounting Policies —

IFRS 16 and COVID-19

Lack of Exchangeability (Amendments to IAS 21) —

Research projects

Dynamic Risk Management —

Pension Benefits That Depend on Asset Returns —

Postimplementation Review of IFRS 10, IFRS 11, and IFRS 12

Other projects

IFRS Taxonomy Update — 2020 General Improvements and Common Practice —

IFRS Taxonomy Update — Amendments to IAS 1, IAS 8, and IFRS Practice Statement 2

This is a substantial amount of information and accountants must ensure that the financial statements they construct or report upon comply with the most recent requirements of the IASB.

International Plus

The United Kingdom and members of the European Union have adopted IASs. It is the country that decides to adopt IASs and the IASB has no authority to govern financial reporting in any country. As well as complying with the requirements of the IASB, the United Kingdom has a very strong legislative body, the Financial Reporting Council (FRC), which regulates auditors, accountants, and actuaries. The FRC is responsible for the United Kingdom's Corporate Governance and Stewardship Codes. The council promotes transparency and integrity in business for investors and others who rely on company reports, audit, and high-quality risk management.

It is also the practice of some companies to provide significantly more financial information required by IFRSs. For our example, we have selected GlaxoSmithKline PLC which was incorporated as an English public limited company on December 6, 1999, through a merger between Glaxo Wellcome PLC and SmithKline Beecham PLC. Their shares are listed on the London Stock Exchange and the NYSE. Their annual report is 304 pages in length and can be downloaded. It has the following main sections:

Strategy Report
Corporate Governance
Remuneration Report
Financial Statements
Investor Information

In the beginning of the report, the company clearly states as follows.

Non-IFRS Measures

We use a number of adjusted, non-IFRS, measures to report the performance of our business. Total reported results represent the Group's overall performance under IFRS. Adjusted results, pro-forma growth rates and other non-IFRS measures may be considered in addition to, but not as a substitute for or superior to, information presented in accordance with IFRS. Adjusted results and other non-IFRS measures are defined on pages 51 to 53 and reconciliations to the nearest IFRS measures are on pages 64 and 68.

On page 53, with other topics, the company refers specifically to exchange rates and explains:

In order to illustrate underlying performance, it is the Group's practice to discuss its results in terms of constant exchange rate (CER) growth. This represents growth calculated as if the exchange rates used to determine the results of overseas companies in Sterling had remained unchanged from those used in the comparative period. CER% represents growth at constant exchange rates. £% or AER% represents growth at actual exchange rates.

This disclosure is not a requirement of any IAS and the company is providing more financial information than that required by IASs.

Blockages and Hurdles

All attempts to create a better financial world, or at least some part of it, are bound to encounter problems. Two, although there are likely more, that have challenged the standard setters have been the Conceptual Framework and the issue of inflation. The Conceptual Framework is intended to serve as a basis for developing financial accounting standards. In the next section, we describe the attempts at developing a framework and its impact. This is followed by the final section of this chapter, which focuses on inflation accounting.

The Conceptual Framework

It is generally agreed that accounting standards would be improved if there were a Conceptual Framework to assist the standard setters. Such a framework would identify the theoretical principles that form the basis for the regulations of financial accounting and reporting. Those involved with standard setting, whether nationally or internationally, have complained that their efforts were made more difficult by the absence of a framework. A specific accounting problem could arise, and an accounting standard would be issued to address it, but unfortunately, this may create conflict with other regulatory guidance, with no coherence and linking of the individual standards.

Setting accounting standards is not the only business activity that requires a Conceptual Framework. A very informative article by Driel (2019) reviews publications in business history and constructs a Conceptual Framework for researching fraud and other dubious financial practices, their determinants, and their consequences. Even when we concentrate on a Conceptual Framework for accounting, there are different views. Gornik-Tomaszewski and Choi (2018) conduct a thorough analysis of the efforts of the FASB and the IASB in developing their own Conceptual Frameworks.

It is argued that the U.S. framework was mainly concerned with the functioning of the capital markets (Barker and Teixeira 2018). At the international level, the IASB has had to consider practices in many countries, which had different histories, industries, and ways of working. The IASC issued its framework in April 1989, and this was adopted by the IASB in 2001. A revised Conceptual Framework was issued in March 2018 by the IASB and was effective immediately. The revised Conceptual Framework is effective for annual reporting periods beginning on or after January 1, 2020, with earlier application permitted. There have been attempts by the United States and the IASB to agree on one converged Conceptual Framework but agreement has not been reached. Both frameworks are amended from time to time and the present preachments by FASB are on the following website: www.fasb.org/jsp/FASB/Page/PreCodSectionPage&cid=1176156317989.

A useful article by Walton (2018) comments on papers comparing the two approaches and an interesting approach by Baker (2017) discusses the influence of accounting theory on the FASB's Conceptual Framework.

Accounting for Inflation

We discussed in Chapter 1 the problem on inflation on financial record keeping and reporting. In the final section of this chapter, we emphasize that the problem continues and there appears to be no solution which is generally acceptable. For several years, the following two approaches to dealing with accounting for inflation have been discussed but not implemented.

Current Purchasing Power (CPP)

With this method, both <u>monetary items</u> and nonmonetary items are separated with different accounting treatments for each. The accounting adjustment for monetary items is subject to the recording of a net gain or <u>loss</u>. Nonmonetary items (those that do not carry a fixed value) are updated into figures with a conversion factor equivalent to price index at the end of the period divided by price index at the date of transaction.

Current Cost Accounting (CCA)

The CCA method values assets at their present fair market value (FMV). This differs significantly from the current method of using the price incurred during the purchase of the fixed asset. With this method, both monetary and nonmonetary items are restated to current values.

The debate on accounting for inflation flourished in the 1970s and 1980s with no final acceptable solution applicable to all companies being reached. In 1979, FASB issued Statement Number 33 Financial Reporting and Changing Prices. This applied to public enterprises that had either inventories and property, plant, and equipment valued at no more than $125 million or total assets amounting to more than $1 billion (after deducting accumulated depreciation). The information required by the statement should be presented as supplementary information in the published annual reports and changes should not be made in the primary financial statements.

In April 2001, the IASB adopted IAS 29 *Financial Reporting in Hyperinflationary Economies*, which had originally been issued by the IASC in July 1989. The standard applies where an entity's functional currency is that of a hyperinflationary economy. The standard does not prescribe when hyperinflation arises but requires the financial statements (and corresponding figures for previous periods) of an entity with hyperinflationary to be restated for the changes in the general pricing power of the functional currency. The standard states that hyperinflation is indicated by factors such as prices, interest, and wages linked to a price index, and cumulative inflation over three years of around 100 percent or more.

The history to the approaches by the United States and the United Kingdom has been well documented by Norby (1980). A thorough analysis of the deliberations in the United States are given by Cohen (1982), and Whittington (2015) comments that "after more than a century of debate, it is not possible to predict the complete disappearance of any of the alternative current valuation methods, and, after half a century of revolution and counterrevolution, HC looks to be remarkably robust." It would seem that despite the many efforts made to account for inflation, Whittington's opinion on the strength of historical costing is appropriate.

Conclusions

The failure to establish IASs that are adopted fully by all countries suggests that there are substantial differences regarding those who are the intended recipients of the financial information and the type of information they require. It is important to remember that it is the country that decides whether it should adopt IASs completely or in part and to which types of companies those standards should apply. The country can also regulate other company activities and our example of the Financial Reporting Committee in the United Kingdom illustrates this. Undoubtedly, the decision by the United States not to adopt IASs and to continue to establish its own is a blow to thoughts of complete internationalization.

The key question is whether IASs improve financial reporting. The authors of an extensive Australian study concluded that financial reports are significantly lengthier; yet are more readable in the post-IFRS period. Also, the length of disclosures in Summary of Significant Accounting Policies, Financial Instruments, and Intangible Assets is significantly longer after the adoption of IFRS (Cheung and Lau 2016). However, it should not be deduced from the above study that the national policies themselves have been changed. The evidence from a Romanian study (Istrate 2015) is that no such changes have taken place.

After years of debate, we can claim that international accounting has been established, but it is only a basic framework. Some countries, and the United Kingdom being a good example, have built their own superstructure. This has resulted in those interested in corporate financial information to have a base for comparisons but the conclusion must be that international differences still exist. Unfortunately, the decision of the United States not to follow international standards detracts from their status. There are no indications that the United States will change its decision.

CHAPTER 3

Developments in the United States

Introduction

The formation of the Securities and Exchange Commission (SEC) can be traced back to the 1930s. The stock market collapse in 1929 destroyed public confidence in the financial markets. It has been contended that, among other factors, one reason for the crash was the poor state of economic intelligence (Galbraith 2009). Investors, both large and small, banks, and financial institutions lost large sums of money. There was a consensus that for the economy to recover, the public's faith in the capital markets needed to be restored. It fell to Congress to identify the problems and recommend solutions. In 1933, the Securities Act was passed and this was followed in 1934 by the Securities Exchange Act, which created the SEC as a government oversight agency responsible for regulating the securities markets and protecting investors. The SEC can bring civil actions against lawbreakers and also works with the Justice Department on criminal cases. The first task for the SEC on its formation was to restore investor confidence in the capital markets by providing investors and the markets with more reliable financial information and clear rules of honest dealing.

In this chapter, we explain first the standard setting process in the United States and the role of the SEC and the Financial Accounting Standards Board (FASB). The major part of the chapter discusses the attempts to converge U.S. standards with the International Accounting Standards. We conclude the chapter by examining the present practices in the United States and the differences with the international approach and also the role of Generally Accepted Accounting Practices (GAAP) in today's financial world.

The Securities and Exchange Commission

Establishing the SEC

The SEC has been in business for over 80 years and the establishment and development of the organization is provided by Atkins and Bondi (2008). It is now a large organization with 4,200 employees with a responsibility for approximately 11,000 investment advisers, 9,700 mutual funds and ETFs, and 4,600 broker-dealers with more than 160,000 branch offices. The SEC is also responsible for reviewing the disclosures and financial statements of more than 12,000 publicly traded companies. It is also responsible for interpreting and enforcing federal securities law and issuing new rules and amending existing rules. It also conducts the inspection of securities firms, brokers, investment advisers, and rating agencies as well as private regulatory organizations in the securities, accounting, and auditing fields. It is fair to say that the SEC has a dominant presence in the U.S. financial world.

It is important to appreciate the connection between the SEC, other government bodies, and financial accounting standards. The SEC enforces U.S. GAAP as developed by the FASB to ensure that issuers are meeting their financial reporting obligations under the federal securities laws. Unfortunately, fraud in business is not unusual in any country. The cases of fraud make the headlines when they are discovered and Marks and Jolicoeur (2010) provide stories of fraud in the United States and the organizations affected at that time.

The governing bodies in the United States, as with other countries, have been aware of the dangers of financial fraud and a lengthy report based on research was issued in October 1987 by the National Commission on Fraudulent Financial Reporting. The SEC has always been alert to various aspects of financial fraud and in 2013 announced three methods to help combat fraud. These were:

- The Financial Reporting and Audit (FRAud) Task Force dedicated to detecting fraudulent or improper financial reporting, whose work will enhance the division's ongoing enforcement efforts related to accounting and disclosure fraud

- The Microcap Fraud Task Force targeting abusive trading and fraudulent conduct in securities issued by microcap companies, especially those that do not regularly publicly report their financial results
- The Center for Risk and Quantitative Analytics employing quantitative data and analysis to profile high-risk behaviors and transactions and support initiatives to detect misconduct, increasing the division's ability to investigate and prevent conduct that harms investors

The SEC established an Enforcement Division's FRAud group to identify and prosecute securities law violations related to financial reporting and audit failures. In 2019, the remit of the group was expanded to investigate areas susceptible to fraudulent financial reporting. These efforts include an ongoing review of financial statement restatements and revisions, an analysis of performance trends by industry, and the use of technology-based tools.

SEC Filings

An SEC filing is a formal document that the SEC requires from certain groups and individuals. There are many such documents depending on the circumstances. Those companies with securities that are publicly traded are required to disclose information on an ongoing basis. Public companies (other than small business issuers) are obliged to submit annual reports on Form 10-K, quarterly reports on Form 10-Q, and current reports on Form 8-K for a number of specified events and must comply with a variety of other disclosure requirements. The Form 10-K, which should be filed with the SEC, contains very detailed information about the company's financial activities for the year. The SEC has adopted a system of disclosure rules for smaller companies filing periodic reports and registration statements. The rules are scaled to reflect the characteristics and needs of smaller companies and their investors.

The SEC has immense authority in ensuring compliance with U.S. GAAP. One could argue that the reason for the formation of the SEC is the reason that U.S. GAAP has developed in the way that it has with accounting principles, standards, and procedures established by a body separate from the SEC and that body is the FASB. Public companies in the United States must follow GAAP when their accountants compile their financial statements. GAAP is a combination of authoritative standards (set by policy boards) and the commonly accepted ways of recording and reporting accounting information.

The Financial Accounting Standards Board

Establishing the FASB

The FASB was founded in 1973 following the recommendations of the 1972 Wheat Committee. The FASB was a different type of organization from its predecessor, the Accounting Principles Board (APB), which was controlled by the accounting profession. The FASB is accountable to the SEC and had the responsibility of acting in the best interests of the main financial statement users. Although discussions take place on the boundaries of its responsibility, the main financial statement users are usually considered to be the investors in companies.

The FASB is authorized by the SEC. This is an unusual relationship as the FASB is a private-sector organization but under the careful surveillance of the SEC. The accounting standards issued by the FASB are recognized as authoritative and generally accepted for purposes of U.S. federal securities laws. In 2009, the FASB ASC (Accounting Standards Codification) was launched and now FASB Accounting Standards Updates (ASUs) are issued to amend the codification. It would be fair to note that the FASB was established and has continued to do its work through some troubled times as noted by Kolton (1982).

The FASB is part of a structure that is independent of all other business and professional organizations, but it is intended that the structure involves interested bodies such as the Government Accounting Standards Board (GASB).

The GASB was established in 1984 to set standards of financial accounting and reporting for state and local governmental units. As with the FASB, the board is responsible for selecting its members, ensuring adequate funding, and exercising general oversight. The Government Accounting Standards Advisory Council (GASAC) has the responsibility for advising the GASB on technical issues on the board's agenda, project priorities, matters likely to require the attention of the GASB, and such other matters as may be requested by the GASB or its chairman.

The FASB Standards-Setting Process

It has been questioned whether the FASB has been able to act independently in setting standards, and an article by Lee (2006) argues that the strategies outlined by the FASB in 2002 to develop a Conceptual Framework would be no more than a short-term palliative to the long-term ills of financial accounting worldwide. A later article by Miller and Bahnson (2013) gives a brief and useful history of the development of the FASB from its inception and the authors contend that it was politically dominated one way or another for virtually its entire existence. They suggest that greater freedom in action occurred from 2013 when it became possible for it to fulfill its social responsibility to help create more efficient capital markets through improved financial reporting.

Whether the failure of the United States to adopt international standards reflects a reluctance to introduce changes is debatable; the present system of standard setting is well established. The stages of the process commence with the board of FASB identifying financial reporting issues based on requests or recommendations from stakeholders or through other means. The board deliberates, at one or more public meetings, the reporting issues identified and analyzed by the staff. Following these investigations, there may be a discussion paper (DP) issued to obtain comments in the project's early stages. The penultimate stage is when the board issues an exposure draft (ED) to solicit broad stakeholder input. Finally, the board issues an ASU describing amendments to the ASC. Updates are published for all authoritative U.S. GAAP released by the FASB and updates will also be issued for amendments to the SEC content in the FASB codification, as well as for editorial changes.

GAAP

The FASB ASC is now the official source of authoritative, nongovernmental GAAP (also known as U.S. GAAP). The purpose of introducing the codification was to order and structure thousands of pronouncements issued by the FASB, the AICPA, and other standards-setting bodies. The structure of the codification is in three tiers. Each topic contains at least one subtopic containing sections that include the actual accounting guidance. Sections are based on the nature of the content, for example, scope, recognition, and measurement. Each section includes numbered paragraphs commencing with the section number followed by the unique paragraph number. PricewaterhouseCoopers has issued a "FASB Accounting Standards Codification Quick Reference Guide," which is easily accessible on their website.

The date of a financial year can differ internationally. A fiscal or financial year is a period for calculating the annual (yearly) financial statements. In many countries, regulatory laws regarding accounting and taxation require such reports once every 12 months, but do not require that the period reported on is a calendar year (i.e., January 1 to December 31). Some companies choose to end their fiscal year on the same day of the week, such a day being the one closest to a particular date. However, the fiscal year is identical to the calendar year for about 65 percent of publicly traded companies in the United States and for a majority of large companies in the United Kingdom. The amount of information that a publicly traded company makes available can be overwhelming and takes many forms. The websites of some companies include so much information that it would need one month to study it.

Electronic Data-Gathering, Analysis, and Retrieval

All companies, foreign and domestic, are required to file registration statements, periodic reports, and other forms electronically through the Electronic Data-Gathering, Analysis, and Retrieval (EDGAR) system. Anyone can access and download information from the system for free. Companies must send annual reports to their shareholders. Under the proxy rules as set out by the SEC, reporting companies are required to post their proxy materials, including their annual reports, on their company websites.

Companies sometimes elect to send their Form 10-K to their shareholders in lieu of providing shareholders with an annual report. The 10-K is required by Section 13 or 15(d) of the Securities Exchange Act of 1934 (the "Act") for which no other form is prescribed.

This form is also the method for transition reports filed in compliance to Section 13 or 15(d) of the Act. Some companies may submit their annual reports electronically in the SEC's EDGAR database. A research study by Chen and Zhou (2019) concludes that XBRL facilitates bulk downloading and processing of company disclosures, suggesting greater information acquisition subsequent to enactment of the XBRL mandate.

Corporate Disclosures

In addition to complying with regulations, many large companies will have a website and also a published report which contains financial information but is also a promotional document. The Amazon Annual Report for 2020 is 75 pages in length. Walmart has a website including a wide range of information and their annual report for 2020 is over 90 pages in length. Walt Disney is even longer and we show below the main items listed on their contents page.

The Walt Disney Company and Subsidiaries Table of Contents

ITEM 1. Business Risk Factors, Unresolved Staff Comments

ITEM 2. Properties

ITEM 3. Legal Proceedings

ITEM 4. Mine Safety Disclosures, Executive Officers of the Company

ITEM 5. Market for the Company's Common Equity, Related Stockholder Matters and Issuer Purchases of Equity Securities

ITEM 6. Selected Financial Data

ITEM 7. Management's Discussion and Analysis of Financial Condition and Results of Operations

ITEM 7A. Quantitative and Qualitative Disclosures About Market Risk

ITEM 8. Financial Statements and Supplementary Data

ITEM 9. Changes in and Disagreements With Accountants on Accounting and Financial Disclosure

ITEM 9A. Controls and Procedures

ITEM 9B. Other Information

PART III

ITEM 10. Directors, Executive Officers and Corporate Governance

ITEM 11. Executive Compensation

ITEM 12. Security Ownership of Certain Beneficial Owners and Management and Related Stockholder Matters

ITEM 13. Certain Relationships and Related Transactions, and Director Independence

ITEM 14. Principal Accounting Fees and Services

PART IV

ITEM 15. Exhibits and Financial Statement Schedules

ITEM 16. Form 10-K Summary, SIGNATURES

Consolidated Financial Information—The Walt Disney Company

You will find that some companies are now including on their website information that comes under the general heading of ESG (environmental, social, and governance). These three aspects of corporate activities are considered to be of interest for "socially responsible investors" who wish their concerns to be reflected into their selection of investments instead of simply considering the potential profitability and/or risk presented by an investment opportunity. We discuss these issues in Chapter 5.

It is noteworthy that the FASB issued on March 19, 2021, a staff educational paper entitled "Intersection of Environmental, Social, and Governance Matters With Financial Accounting Standards." The paper does not change or modify current GAAP and is not intended to be a comprehensive assessment of the intersection of ESG matters with financial accounting standards. The paper discusses the following three topics and is a potential marker to the way that accounting standards may develop in the future. The three topics the paper discusses are:

Overview of ESG Reporting

The FASB's Role in Setting Financial Accounting Standards

Intersection of ESG Matters With Financial Accounting Standards

The paper recognizes that ESG issues extend over a broad range of topics, which are beyond the topics covered by financial accounting standards. However, the paper recognizes some ESG issues may have a material direct or indirect effect on the financial statements and that in some industries environmental matters, if material, may be an input to many accounting measurements.

The Broken Honeymoon

In establishing the International Accounting Standards Board, it was assumed generally that the involvement of the United States was required to provide legitimacy and to make it truly "international." In this section, we discuss the first stages of the relationship—the honeymoon. In subsequent sections, we explain the gradual breaking up of the relationship.

In the early years, there was every indication, at least publicly, that the International Accounting Standards Committee (IASC) and the FASB were working toward an agreement. Possibly, the most encouraging event was the signing, in 2002, by both parties of the Norwalk Agreement, which had the objective of converging U.S. standards and international standards.

Although discussions and agreements continued for several years, some critics would claim there were early indications, as we discuss in the following sections, that complete agreement would not be reached. In retrospect, one could argue that there was little chance that an agreement could be reached, but it took some years for the application and implication of internationalization to be understood fully. This was possibly most apparent in establishing standards for leasing and financial instruments and we discuss these issues at the end of this section on the broken honeymoon.

The Engagement

The lengthy and arduous progress of the relationship between the United States and international standard setters has been extremely well researched and described by Kirsch (2012). It was not until 1988 when the IASC had issued nearly 30 separate international standards that the FASB publicly announced its position on international accounting. It stated that its intention was to support the development of superior international standards that would then gradually supplant national standards as the superior standards became universally accepted.

The FASB stated its opinion that it could contribute to the improvement of international standards in many ways. In 1991, it published an authoritative article on its plans for international activities, which was based on two key assumptions. The first assumption was that domestic financial reporting needs would continue to be the FASB's first priority. The second assumption was that its international activities would be conducted within its charter and mission statement. Critics would suggest that this carefully phrased expression of involvement did not suggest an overwhelming intent to adopt international accounting but more a move toward shaping it to meet the needs of the United States.

Although the United States had been a supporter of international accounting since 1973, the event that increased the interest and enthusiasm in international accounting was possibly the Sarbannes–Oxley (SOX) Act of 2002. This was a regulatory response to the substantial financial frauds and accounting irregularities that had occurred in companies such as Enron, WorldCom, and Tyco. These highly publicized financial collapse of these companies raised doubt on the rigor of U.S. standard setting and the disclosure requirements placed on companies. It is probable that they also encouraged the FASB to look more closely at the development of financial regulations. These frauds by major companies have been well documented and Hays and Ariail (2013) provide an insight into the Enron case.

As the years passed, the United States became more closely involved in the development of International Financial Reporting Standards (IFRSs) issued by the International Accounting Standards Board and, at the same time, changed parts of its own regulations so that they complemented the international approach to accounting issues. This involvement did not necessarily signal the intention to adopt the total of IFRSs that had already been issued in their original format. It was an offer to cooperate with the IASB in developing standards that both boards found acceptable.

The FASB suggestions for greater international involvement were met with enthusiasm by the IASC. It was difficult for the IFRSs to identify the standards they issued as international when the largest financial market—the United States—did not adopt them. The expression of greater involvement by the United States raised the reputation of international standards. There was also the possibility that the involvement of the United States in international accounting would encourage other countries to follow the same route. In 1996, the SEC indicated that it supported the IASC's objective to develop accounting standards that could be accepted when preparing the necessary financial statements in cross-border offerings.

The IASC sought to establish a set of comprehensive, generally accepted accounting pronouncements, which were of high quality and resulted in three elements: comparability, transparency, and full disclosure for users. If these qualities could be captured by the IASC, it was the SEC's intention to consider permitting foreign issuers offering securities in the United States to draw up their financial statements by applying international standards. Such a move undoubtedly would increase interest in several countries on the advantages of international accounting standards.

There is a word of caution, however, as although the SEC and the FASB expressed their support for international accounting they also realized that, if both a quality IAS setting structure and process were established, it might lead to structural and procedural changes to the FASB, as well as potential changes in its national role. The FASB would lose its position and no longer be the accounting rule setter in the United States. However, the FASB intended to retain its position and stated that it intended to retain its worldwide leadership role in standard setting and believed that "Worldwide acceptance of internationally recognized standards and a global standard-setting process is impossible without U.S. acceptance and participation" (FASB 1999).

The IASB was established formally in April 2001. In 2002, the recently appointed chair of the IASB, David Tweedie, made clear his aim of spreading IASs to the United States. It was realized that it was unlikely for the United States to adopt the already existing IFRSs in one sweep. A possible path was to converge IFRSs and U.S. GAAP, by both sides jointly agreeing on changes to the existing standards to produce one set of high-quality, global accounting regulations. An improvement project was suggested as the first step to promote convergence on high-quality standards and the objective was to revise and reissue 12 named IASC standards by the first half of 2003.

The appointment in July 2002 of a new FASB chair, Robert Herz, added a fresh international dimension to the United States' way of thinking. He was a qualified UK chartered accountant and had previously served on the IASB. His appointment brought with it a greater commitment to convergence, which complemented the objectives of the restructured IASB under David Tweedie. The rapport led to the signing in 2002 of the Norwalk Agreement, which had the objective of converging U.S. standards and international standards.

Revisiting the Agreement

The Norwalk Agreement had a substantial impact on the process of "Internationalization." There were events both internal and external to the United States that strengthened the argument for the country being closely involved with international standards. The New York Stock Exchange (NYSE) was facing growing competition from markets in other countries and foreign companies were finding that the U.S. requirements, such as the SOX Act, were becoming increasingly onerous if they were seeking a listing. There had also been a number of well-publicized financial scandals such as Enron and WorldCom. Confidence in U.S. financial reporting regulations and the effectiveness of the rules-based approach to regulation had been eroded.

Other occurrences encouraged the United States to be part of the international accounting framework. Several countries had either adopted international accounting or were planning to do so and the IASB was a much more effective organization than the IASC. There was also greater recognition of international standards on developing capital markets and this threatened New York's claim as the premier capital market. These events focused the attention in the United States to the potential of international accounting and the threat to its own structures if it did not clearly state its intentions. In October 2002, the FASB and the newly formed IASB signed an agreement in Norwalk, Connecticut.

This agreement sets out the aims of the two boards and the actions they intended to take jointly.

The enthusiasm at the time of signing the Norwalk Agreement was substantial and the problems likely to occur were underestimated. Changes to accounting standards are extremely disruptive and expensive as they have an impact on accountants, auditors, investors, and other users of financial statements. Although the two parties claimed that the differences between U.S. GAAP and internationalization were not insurmountable, in practice it appeared that if "the goal of their convergence efforts was common standards, they sometimes fell short of that objective" (Kirsch 2012, 47).

Although the two major accounting standard setters had achieved an agreement, it appears as if it had been forgotten that there were many others who would be affected by any changes to existing international standards. Many countries had adopted international standards and the aim of U.S. convergence would involve changes to their newly established accounting practices. The users of the present financial statements would also need to become accustomed to the new requirements. A further barrier was that auditors would need to become thoroughly familiar with the new requirements.

The United States has been setting accounting standards for over half a century, which had incurred substantial investment and resulted in a highly sophisticated system of accounting regulation. An acceptable and well-used procedure was in place and there did not appear, in some opinions, a good reason to abandon U.S. standards. Although a move to international standards suggests that U.S. regulators wished to cooperate with other major countries on important global business issues and reinforced the reputation of the United States as a global force, there were downsides that needed to be considered. Careful thought suggested complete and full adoption may not be a sensible decision. There could be an alternative approach to full adoption where the involvement of the FASB in international standard setting would ensure that the United States could greatly influence the development of standards. The United States could make a valuable contribution to the improvement of international standards without the SEC and the FASB losing control of their own regulations.

There was the possible risk that if the United States did not fully adopt international standards or play a major role in the formation of multinational corporations, it would find that international standards became firmly established. The result could be that U.S. standards could become an ineffective competitor relative to an increasingly dominant international body. Already, some concerns had been expressed that there had been a significant shift in global market capitalization, with U.S. market share steadily declining.

There are various influences that operate over time to determine the market share of a particular stock exchange, but the data do suggest some erosion in the popularity of the U.S. market. The NYSE market cap at the end of 2003 was 31 times that of Shanghai Exchange. In July 2009, the NYSE was 3.6 times that of Shanghai. According to the September 2009 Standard & Poor report, the U.S. market was less than 41 percent of global capital markets, a substantial decline from January 2004, when it was nearly 53 percent. This process of competition has continued. If we consider the position in early 2021, the following are the top six stock exchanges by market capitalization:

Exchange	Market capitalization (US$B)
New York Stock Exchange	26,230
Nasdaq	19,020
Shanghai Stock Exchange	6,980
Japan Stock Exchange Group	6,640
Hong Kong Stock Exchange	6,130
Euronext	5,440

The NYSE still maintains a very strong position but it is interesting to note that the NYSE allows international companies to list and they can choose between using IFRS in its original IASB version instead of U.S. GAAP.

The Search for Harmony

Attempting Reconciliation

Whether we are concerned with national or international standards, it is accepted that such standards should ensure companies issued financial statements that explained the companies' financial progress or lack of it. In 1997, the then chair of the SEC claimed that standards must result in comparability and transparency, and provide for full disclosure. Investors must be able to meaningfully analyze performance across time periods and among companies. The SEC echoes the words of many others when it states that high-quality accounting standards consist of a comprehensive set of neutral principles that require consistent, comparable, relevant, and reliable information. The information should be useful for investors, lenders, creditors, and others who make capital allocation decisions.

The difficulty is that once the overarching descriptive values are agreed, the qualities of an effective and necessary standard are less apparent. It could be argued that these are the standards that establish high-quality financial statements allowing regulators to monitor and enforce them. It could also be interpreted as standards that require companies to provide information that is of use to the investor. There are several opinions on high quality and Barth, Landsman, Lang, and Williams (2012) conducted a research study that investigated the question of quality. The study compared characteristics of accounting statements for firms that apply International Accounting Standards to a matched sample of firms that did not. The attributes to determine quality were management, timely loss recognition, and value relevance metrics. The findings of their study demonstrated that firms applying international standards use less earnings management, reduce more timely loss recognition, and establish more value relevance of accounting amounts than do those applying domestic GAAP. The conclusion from the study suggests that improvement in accounting quality is associated with applying IAS. We emphasize that this study was not a direct comparison of U.S. and international standards, although it identifies the quality of international standards.

One study does not provide complete answers and is unlikely to persuade policy makers in any particular direction. The research study does demonstrate that the pursuit of high-quality standards requires some measures by which we can assess them. It must also be accepted that standards are not only driven by technical accounting considerations but other powerful influences. In 2017, the chair of the SEC (Whyte 2017) stressed the need for high-quality standards that are globally accepted. If we wish to argue the acceptance of international standards, then U.S. investors should make investment decisions in foreign companies that are using international standards. Also, U.S. companies should make acquisitions, enter into joint ventures, and enter into transactions with foreign companies that use international standards. If international accounting is to be achieved, there must be agreement on the assumptions and concepts that are to serve as the basis for setting standards.

Different Approaches

Unfortunately, the IASB has a very different approach to setting standards compared to that of the United States. The IASB uses a principles-based approach to standard setting; the United States uses a rules-based approach. The difference between a principles-based approach and a rules-based approach is that with the principles-based approach, the burden is placed on the preparers and auditors of the financial statements to use their professional judgment and experience to ensure that the financial statements are not misleading and comply with the conceptual regulations in the standards. The rules-based approach uses the assumption that if the published accounting standards are complied with fully when preparing financial statements, those statements will give faithful representation. To ensure that the rules-based approach provides quality financial statements, the regulations must set out specific criteria, bright line thresholds, examples, scope restrictions, exceptions, subsequent precedents, and implementation guidance (Nelson 2003).

When the differences between the rules-based approach and the principles-based approach are discussed, the importance of a Conceptual Framework that determines the nature of the approach to standard setting is important. An insight to the differences in the accounting approach can be found in the wording of the auditors' statement that accompanies the annual report and accounts. Below we show a brief extract from the audit statement for the documents issued recently by Walmart Inc. in the United States:

> These financial statements are the responsibility of the Company's management. Our responsibility is to express an opinion on the Company's financial statements based on our audits. We are a public accounting firm registered with the PCAOB and are

required to be independent with respect to the Company in accordance with the U.S. federal securities laws and the applicable rules and regulations of the Securities and Exchange Commission and the PCAOB.

As a comparator, we show an extract from the auditor's report for Rio Tinto PLC in the United Kingdom:

the financial statements give a true and fair view of the state of the Group's and of the UK Parent Company's, Rio Tinto plc, affairs as at 31 December 2020, and of the Group's profit for the year then ended; the Group financial statements have been properly prepared in accordance with international accounting standards in conformity with the requirements of the Companies Act 2006, and International Financial Reporting Standards (IFRSs) adopted pursuant to Regulation (EC) No. 1606/2002 as it applies in the European Union ("IFRSs as adopted by the EU").

We have extracted these statements to illustrate the very different approaches adopted by the companies and the auditors in the preparation of financial statements and that difference is in the use of the term "true and fair" which, in turn, is related to the Conceptual Framework. You will not find the term used by any company complying with U.S. accounting standards.

Possibly the first attempt to explain the different approaches to commerce between the United Kingdom and the United States generally has been traced back to 1660 by Ashley (1899). More recently, in December 2020, Vasile and Croitoru (2020) addressed the divide in an article on the financial audit and in the same year Ciocan and Georgescu (2020) considered the subject of true and fair in relation to conservatism in Romania.

The explanation of true and fair has collected many articles over the years and it is an extremely important concept in the setting of international standards. As a concept, it is part of the basis or framework for setting standards but this has proved to be elusive and both the FASB and the IASB are continuing, independently, to establish a Conceptual Framework. Gornik-Tomaszewski and Choi provide a useful explanation of the work that has been taking place and argue that the Conceptual Framework is not only for standard setters, but also to users of financial statements and other stakeholders. Spalding and Lawrie (2019) provide a useful insight into the decision of the American Institute of Certified Public Accountants (AICPA) to promote ethical principles and best practices by adding a "Conceptual Framework" to its existing Code of Professional Conduct.

A study (Chand, Patel, and Day 2008) of four countries identified three dominant factors that are barriers to accounting convergence. These are the nature of business ownership, the financial system, and culture. To some extent, this takes us back to the discussions in 1660. One comes to the conclusion that accounting is far from being an exact science and, in Chapter 1, we discussed the continuing, but still unresolved, issue of accounting for inflation. Some would argue that the failure to resolve this issue exposes the weakness of present accounting methods for measuring and reporting financial performance.

The Beginning of the End

Given our doubts expressed in the last section on the needs for an agreed Conceptual Framework, it is not surprising that the discussions between the United States and the IASB would come to an end. The progress toward convergence from 2002 to 2014 was one of memorandums, road maps, objectives, and milestones. Despite all of these carefully worded documents, full convergence was not achieved and the U.S. GAAP remains firmly in place, although definitely influenced by the events. One interesting development was that foreign companies issuing shares would be permitted to list on the NYSE using IFRS. The SEC adopted this change in 2007 but the question was undoubtedly in many minds that if IFRSs were appropriate for the financial statements of non-U.S. companies, why not for U.S. companies.

In 2008, the United States issued a road map to indicate their future path, which identified a series of priorities and milestones, emphasizing the goal of joint projects to produce common, principle-based standards. It indicated that adoption of IFRS in the United States would be conditional upon the achievement of progress toward certain milestones. These included progress in improvements in accounting, evidence of stable funding that supported the independent functioning of the IASB, and improvement in the use of interactive data for IFRS reporting. The SEC was to consider the state of preparedness of U.S. issuers, auditors, and users, including the availability of IFRS education and training. There was general satisfaction that the United States was moving toward international accounting, but it was refined by its own views.

Unfortunately, the financial crisis of 2007/08 occurred and this event was largely blamed on the inadequacy of accounting regulations to determine the proper accounting treatment for financial instruments. There were requests from many parties, including various government agencies, for the FASB and the IASB to speed up their progress. In response, the IASB and the FASB published a progress report describing an intensification of their work program, including the hosting of monthly joint board meetings and quarterly updates on their progress on convergence projects.

In 2010, the SEC published its Draft Strategic Plan for fiscal years 2010 through 2015. The document includes drafts of the SEC's mission, vision, values, strategic goals, major initiatives, and performance metrics. In the plan, the SEC proposed an objective of promoting high-quality financial reporting worldwide through, among other things, support for a single set of high-quality global accounting standards and promotion of the ongoing convergence initiatives between the FASB and the IASB. The plan also stated that the decision for incorporating IASs in the U.S. financial reporting system would be made in 2011.

The document did not provide any details of potential transition dates or approaches, but the staff stated that 2015 or 2016 seemed reasonable based on comments received on the 2008 IFRS road map. The SEC also indicated that an early adoption was viable if it decided to make the use of IFRS mandatory. In 2012, the IASB and the FASB published a joint progress document in which they described the progress made on an accounting standard for financial instruments. This included a joint expected loss impairment (provisioning) approach and a more converged approach to classification and measurement.

The Final Chapter

The years leading up to the withdrawal of the SEC from international accounting were busy, but a clear view of where the SEC was heading was not known. Undoubtedly, the decision was difficult and, for several years, there had been considerable activity but no clear signs of the position that the SEC intended to adopt. Many thought that the SEC would make a final decision on the adoption of international accounting by 2012.

This did not happen and the opinions of some other major players were that the IASB should cease its relationship with the United States and direct its attention to the rest of the world. The Institute of Chartered Accountants in England and Wales responded to the failure of the SEC to decide on convergence and proposed that the convergence project should be ended formally, in months and not years. The argument was made that the IASB should concern itself with the 100-plus countries that had already adopted international standards. The most important priority was to assist those countries, such as China, which were making moves to convergence (Institute of Chartered Accountants in England and Wales 2012).

Not the Words but Their Use

Disquiet was being expressed not only by those countries that had already adopted international standards but also by the standard setting bodies in the United States and internationally. In 2013, the IASB and the FASB published a high-level update on the status and timeline of the remaining convergence projects. The report includes an update on the impairment phase of the joint project on financial instruments and the FASB made encouraging comments on convergence but there were also doubts expressed. The FASB argued that convergence could be interpreted in different ways. It could mean the discussion between two or more parties leading to complete agreement on one course of action or it could refer to both the intended goal and the path by which to reach it. Its opinion was that the plan was to identify a unified set of high-quality IASs that companies worldwide would use for both domestic and cross-border financial reporting. The FASB wished to participate in developing accounting standards that are as converged as possible without forgoing the quality demanded by U.S. investors and other users of financial statements. This pronouncement was generally interpreted that the United States had decided not to pursue full convergence.

It may not be necessarily the regulations set by the standard setters that are the difficulty, but the environment in which they are being applied, that is, the individual countries where the companies are located and transact business. As long as the standards are considered to be of high quality, it can be argued that it does not matter whether the FASB or the IASB set the standards, but the crucial ingredient is the environment within a country that ensures organizational compliance.

Given the failure of U.S. GAAP and IFRS to converge, the question is: What is the next step? It is evident that the IASB has decided to follow its own path. This does not mean the exclusion of U.S. involvement but full "convergence" is no longer the aim. From the view of the United States, it has an international presence and can influence the further development of international corporate reporting, both financial and nonfinancial.

Although the FASB has not expressed 100 percent enthusiasm for international accounting set by the IASB, there appeared to be expressions of cooperation. There were two issues that revealed the differences between the FASB and the IASB in formulating accounting standards. These were accounting for leases and financial instruments.

Leasing

Leasing is an important activity in the business world. It is a method for obtaining an essential source of funding for companies wishing to acquire or use noncurrent assets. In some taxation jurisdictions, it has been possible to structure agreements so that either, or both, the lessor or lessee enjoy significant taxation benefits.

Both the U.S. standards and the international accounting guidance concentrate on what a capital (finance) lease is and this must be shown on the balance sheet. The original U.S. standard (SFAS 13) defines a capital lease as one under which any one of the following four conditions is met: (1) The present value at the beginning of the lease term of the payments, not representing executory costs, paid by the lessor equals or exceeds

90 percent of the fair value of the leased asset. (2) The lease transfers ownership of the asset to the lessee by the end of the lease term. (3) The lease contains a bargain purchase price. (4) The lease is equal to 75 percent or more of the estimated economic life of the leased asset.

The former international standard, Accounting for Leases (IAS 17), states that the classification of a lease depends on the substance of the transaction, rather than the form. The standard describes situations that would normally lead a lease to be classified as a financing (capital) lease. A guide to the situation where this occurs is provided in the standard.

The above explanation of the two approaches to appropriate accounting standards demonstrates the rules-based approach with its specific, quantitative guidelines and the principles-based approach with its descriptive guidance. These different approaches lead to problems and demonstrate the differences between the two standard setters. With specified rules, professional accounting opinion is not required and the problem is that decisions may be consistent with the rules but inconsistent with the principle of providing the most useful financial information to users. There is also the danger that where the rules are very specific, companies may be able to arrange their activities so that they comply and fall within the rules, but the financial statements still remain misleading.

However, it can be argued that the principles-based approach gives too much scope to preparers and auditors, which creates opportunities for creative accounting. Without clear guidance on how to account for a transaction, several methods may be considered acceptable. Those different methods can lead to different answers, which is not in the best interests of the users of financial statements. A useful article on the FASB's present approach to accounting for leases is given by Casabona and Coville (2018) and an analysis of the approach taken by the IASB is provided by Kabir and Rahman (2018).

Financial Instruments

Classification of a lease depends on whether the lease meets certain criteria. The definition of financial instruments states that there must be a contract and this gives rise to financial assets, financial liabilities, and equity, which appear on a balance sheet. The definition of a financial instrument is also two sided: The contract must always give rise to a financial asset of one party, with a corresponding financial liability or equity instrument of another party.

Financial markets are used by companies to raise finances for their business activities. External financial markets can be considered short term, less than a year, or long term. Short-term financial markets are often called money markets. Long-term financial markets are called capital markets and include the equity market, the debt market, which includes borrowing from other firms, and the bank market. Multinational companies that used to raise equity capital solely from sources within their own country now look to other countries for potential shareholders; this is known as cross-border financing. There are several types of risks associated with using financial markets. There is interest-rate risk from making investments or taking out loans, or exchange-rate risk through international trade.

Companies can attempt to reduce it by hedging the risk. An example of hedging is as follows: A company knows that it has to purchase supplies of materials in three months' time. The materials, such as agricultural crops, may not be ready to be purchased right away, or the company may not wish to hold the materials until they are needed. There is a risk that the price of materials will increase before the end of the three months. The company can enter into an agreement now to purchase the goods in three months' time, but at a current price. The company avoids the risk of the prices increasing in three months' time when it requires the materials. It also loses the opportunity to make a gain if the price decreases in three months' time.

Contracts are used for trading in derivatives. These are commonly traded among financial institutions, individual investors, fund managers, corporations, and private companies. The trades are conducted at either a physical location such as an exchange or remotely in what is termed the over-the-counter market.

Undoubtedly, deciding the accounting treatment for financial instruments causes problems which have been identified by Abdel-Khalik (2019). When the global financial crisis of 2007/08 arose, it caused considerable panic. Understandably, people wanted to know the cause of the crisis, and financial instruments became the focus. The reasons offered for financial instruments being the culprit fell into two main camps. There were those who believed that complex financial instruments had been used inappropriately. Others, particularly the banks, argued that it was not the financial instruments that were to blame but the way that they had to be accounted for by using fair-value accounting. This required valuation of financial assets at their current market value. Thus, fair-value accounting forced companies to write down financial asset values, destroying equity and weakening banks' lending practices. The defenders of fair-value accounting argued that the method was not the cause of the crisis. They claimed that fair value only revealed the effects of poor decisions.

For the FASB and the IASB, the focus on accounting for financial instruments started in March 2006. The boards declared their intentions to work together to improve and converge financial reporting standards by issuing a memorandum of understanding (MoU), *A Roadmap for Convergence Between IFRS and U.S. GAAP—2006–2008*. As part of the MoU, the boards worked jointly on a research project to reduce the complexity of the accounting for financial instruments. The two boards were unable to agree on a joint standard and the failure to do so confirmed that the convergence project was not achievable. In 2012, the FASB and the IASB tried to resolve their differences, but finally decided to develop their own standards. The IASB continued its work in separate phases whereas the FASB initially decided to issue one ED for comment. In 2014, the IASB published the complete version of IFRS 9 *Financial Instruments*, which replaces most of the guidance in IAS 39. In 2016, the FASB issued Accounting Standards Update 2016-01, *Financial Instruments—Overall: Recognition and Measurement of Financial Assets and Financial Liabilities.*

The Divorce

In 2010, it seemed that the convergence project was on a sound course. However, there were examples where the two parties had not been able to reach a full convergence. Although neither the FASB nor the IASB had made any public declarations, there was an obvious decline in the U.S. enthusiasm. It was not surprising that, in 2014, the FASB argued that the objective for international accounting standards could be achieved in different ways.

The FASB suggested that the original aim of convergence was to develop a unified set of high-quality international standards. This did not necessarily mean that the two parties had to issue a single standard to which they were both committed fully. To achieve converged standards, the FASB considered a better route was to work on global issues with the IASB and other countries through membership of the Accounting Standards Advisory Forum (ASAF). The reference by the FASB to high-quality standards appeared to weaken the chance of further convergence between the two bodies. The foundation of the disagreement can be traced to the rules versus principles debate.

The rules-based approach lays down specific, detailed requirements in a standard to ensure that financial statements do not mislead the users. Most would agree that the FASB inclines toward this method for setting its standards. Critics would claim that the rules-based approach can result in financial statements that are consistent with the rules but do not always provide the most reliable and relevant information for users. Strict conformity with the rules may fail to capture fully the complexities of business operations.

The principles-based approach sets out the general boundaries of the standard's requirements. It is the preparers and auditors who apply their professional judgment and experience to ensure that the financial statements do not mislead the users. It can be argued that this approach gives too much scope to preparers and auditors to select various methods for recording accounting transactions.

It should not be concluded that there will be no further cooperation between the FASB and the IASB and some acceptance of the standards set by the other body. The present position suggests that the FASB and the IASB will retain the responsibility for issuing their own standards. It may be that the two sets of standards will be similar but U.S. GAAP will remain under the control of the SEC and the FASB, and international standards will remain the domain of the IASB. An interesting development was that, beginning in fiscal 2007, the U.S. SEC allowed foreign companies to trade on U.S. stock exchanges to report under IFRS or U.S. GAAP.

Perhaps convergence will be resurrected. The similarity of the two sets of standards for sophisticated users of financial statements has already been established. One study (Jategaonkar, Lovata, and Sierra 2014) concluded that the predictive models employed by analysts are equally effective when based on financial results reported under U.S. GAAP or IFRS.

A Reconciliation?

Given the many years that were spent by the United States and the IASB in attempting to achieve an agreement, there is the question whether an agreement may still be reached. At the time of writing this book, there are no indications of the convergence project being revived. It would seem that the FASB and the IASB will retain the responsibility for issuing their own standards. International standards will remain the domain of the IASB. The similarity of the two sets of standards for sophisticated users of financial statements has already been established.

There are several articles that examine the experiences of countries outside the United States that have adopted IFRSs instead of maintaining their own standard setting process. De Luca and Prather-Kinsey (2018) use legitimacy theory to determine whether one set of global accounting standards is feasible and argue that currently democratic processes of national standard setters impede the global "adoption" of IASB. They consider that adoption of IFRS worldwide is possible and to achieve this IOSCO could become the international regulator. Their view is not shared by everyone and Ray (2018) from his studies concludes that there is an academic skepticism toward a "one size fits all" approach to accounting standards.

An examination of opinions outside of the main decision makers in the FASB and the IASB suggest that convergence will never be achieved. Elam (2020) applying a social mood perspective argues the probability of an agreement was in doubt from the beginning. One could assume that there have been no activities from either party to suggest that future convergence appears possible.

Managers, financial analysts, investors, lenders, compensation committees, and other stakeholders often evaluate a company's earnings performance using metrics other than GAAP-based net income. These stakeholders generally start with GAAP earnings and back out (or exclude) earnings components that they deem to be transitory or noncash. They argue that these excluded items are less relevant for assessing firm performance and that the "non-GAAP" performance number is more appropriate for their intended purposes. The growth in these non-GAAP metrics over the past 20 years reflects a widespread acceptance of non-standard performance metrics as a way to evaluate firm performance.

A Non-GAAP World

The main thrust of this chapter has been the tension between the U.S. GAAP and the International Accounting Standards. Black, Christensen, Ciesielski, and Whipple (2018) argue that worldwide GAAP is difficult to achieve and, from their own research, argue that the dynamic landscape of non-GAAP reporting will grow. It should also be emphasized that GAAP is restricted to a relatively few business organizations and all businesses in the United States do not follow GAAP. It is not a statutory requirement for all U.S. businesses. Publicly traded companies must comply with GAAP, and private businesses and other organizations may elect to use GAAP because investors, analysts, and others are interested in the financial position of a business.

Managers, financial analysts, investors, lenders, and others interested in a business may choose to use standards other than GAAP. They revise the earnings calculated under GAAP to meet their own interests. An extensive study by Henry, Weitz, and Rosenthal (2020) reviewed the fourth-quarter earnings releases of the S&P 100 for the years 2010 through 2016, studying the extent and nature of non-GAAP reporting by large public companies and the impact of changing SEC regulation and guidance. One of their findings was that there was an increase in the number of companies reporting non-GAAP earnings, which reached 72 percent by 2016.

From the research available, it would appear that public companies may comply with GAAP but also take the opportunity in their annual reports to provide substantial non-GAAP information. It is only reasonable to point out that the publication of non-GAAP measures is not only found under U.S. regulations. An Australian study by Malone, Tarca, Wee, and Cahan (2016) concluded from their research that analysts are active in adjusting IFRS earnings to arrive at a number that is more useful for assessing current performance and predicting future earnings, and that companies assist in this process by their estimation of the adjustments required. The authors concluded from their research that the practice produced useful information.

Conclusions

In discussing the developments in the United States, we have possibly separated their experiences from the events internationally. We agree with Dennis (2019) that there are still important questions about the Conceptual Framework that need to be answered before an adequate framework can be constructed. The leap from that stage to developing accounting standards acceptable to all countries may be too great a step. There is also the issue that the attention is mainly focused on the agreement between the United States and the IASB. We examined the scope of international accounting in Chapter 2 and it would be fair to conclude that the adoption of IFRSs by individual countries has raised challenges for many.

In contemplating the possibility of the FASB and the IASB in achieving an agreement, the experience demonstrates that this is highly unlikely. One additional piece of evidence that confirms this opinion is not concerned with private companies but public sector accounting standards. Research by Pollanen (2020) concentrated on the United States and Canada. Although numerous European countries have adopted the International Public Sector Accounting Standards, she argues that there is an apparent embedded belief in the United States that its rules-based national standards are superior to the principles-based IFRSs and the International Public Sector Accounting Standards. The references to the various barriers there are to convergence suggest that the United States will retain control of its own accounting regulations. The conclusion must be that convergence has come to an end.

CHAPTER 4

Islamic Accounting

Introduction

Islam is the second largest religion in the world, with 1.9 billion followers representing more than 24 percent of the world's population. Muslims adhere to Islamic law (Sharia) in their day-to-day behavior. To the Muslim community, Islam is a way of life as it governs all aspects of life. The influence of religion on accounting is not a new phenomenon and has been explored to a great extent in the literature. In Islam, accounting if performed in accordance with the Sharia should be no different than other acts of worship. It has been argued that Sharia affects the view of the accounting conceptual framework (Gambling and Karim 1991; Shihadah 1987; Zaid 1995). In the holy book of Islam (*the Qur'an*), the word "hesab" or (account) is mentioned more than eight times in different verses (Askary and Clarke 1997). The reference here is to account to God on all matters pertaining to human endeavor for which every Muslim is "accountable."

Islamic accounting is still a relatively new concept. It is highly recognized by Muslim accountants throughout the world and it developed because of economic changes since the late 1960s. These changes substantially increased the wealth held by Muslims, particularly in the Middle East. The creation of Islamic banks and other financial institutions, coupled with their international expansion and the growth of Islamic financial institutions in the last four decades, has increased the complexities and sophistication of transactions and contributed to creating the need for Islamic accounting. Another factor for the increased popularity of Islamic accounting is the development of universities in Muslim countries. There are currently 1,840 universities and degree awarding institutes in the Muslim world. Several universities in countries like Malaysia, Pakistan, and Turkey have Islamic research centers.

The growth of Islamic financial institutions has drawn the attention of regulators, practitioners, and investors, which ensures the maintenance of certain regulations, standards, and good practices (Hassan and Aliyu 2018; Hassan, Aliyu, and Hussain 2019). Relatively few studies covering accounting in Muslim countries have appeared in English-language journals. In this chapter, we examine the principles that govern Islamic accounting; similarities and differences between Islamic accounting and IFRS; and the implications of zakat (charitable donations) and interest on Islamic accounting.

International Accounting Versus Islamic Principles

One of the most important objectives of financial reporting from an Islamic viewpoint is for users to be able to assess whether the entity is abiding by the "principles of Sharia." While Muslim scholars stress that accounting should provide information to enable its users to make informed decisions, they argue that the objectives of the information on Islamic institutions are much wider than conventional approaches to accounting. These different opinions on the basic purpose of accounting lead to controversy. Triyuwono (2000) argues that any accounting policy must comply with the Islamic Sharia, and, the enterprise would be encouraged to participate in releasing humans from the oppression of economic, social, and intellectual factors and environment exploitation. Shahul and Yaya (2003) claim that conventional accounting provides only partial information for making the various decisions by the users but ignores important information relating to disclosure of the environmental affects, social costs, and other religious transactions of an entity. Islamic accounting provides all the information including social, environmental, and religious transactions as per their accountability and justice to the related parties and also as per their accountability to God.

Many global financial institutions have adopted International Financial Reporting Standards (IFRSs). In early 2021, approximately 120 countries either permit or require IFRS for domestic listed companies. Clearly, there are potential economic and practical benefits for Islamic institutions to follow the IFRS regulations. One of these benefits is providing users with transparency as part of a reasonably comprehensive and well-understood accounting framework. The additional pressure on Islamic financial institutions is that many operate outside the Muslim world and they were obliged to follow IFRS. The question arises on how serious these differences are and whether there is a solution which satisfies all parties.

The Conflict Between Zakat and IFRS

Zakat has been described as the cornerstone of the financial structure in an Islamic State (Siddiqi 1982). Muslim sole proprietors and partners are obliged to pay zakat on both personal wealth and business profits (Faris 1966). For payment of zakat, the assets must possess the characteristics which are (a) full ownership, (b) asset is growing or productive, (c) assets above the basic requirement, and (d) owned for a full year. For calculation of zakat, valuation of assets should be according to the current market price or net realizable value. Inventories valuation should not be the lower amount of cost or market price or there should not be maintained any allowance for doubtful accounts receivable (Clarke, Craig, and Hamid 1996).

One of the pillars of Islam is the payment of zakat. The classification of assets and liabilities in the balance sheet should be disclosed in such a way that identifies what wealth is, subject to zakat. The valuation of current assets based on current market values will lead to the recognition in financial statements of the difference between cost and market values; this difference is taxable according to Sharia, but not distributable. Accounting in Islam is viewed as a tool that enables the proper calculation of zakat.

The key distinction of Islamic accounting is that the concepts of conservatism and historical cost are not relevant for Islamic financial reporting purposes and the calculation of zakat. Advocates of Islamic accounting argue that, unlike IFRS, which relies on a strong framework of principles that emphasize the economic nature of transactions in Islam, the contractual aspect of the transaction is crucial for Sharia compliance. Under those contracts are Sharia principles which forbid Riba (interest). Islam claims "money should not beget money," that is, in order for money to earn a permissible return, it must be used in real economic activity

(Sydney Homer 1963). The focus of Islamic accounting is on profit while IFRS focuses on interest which is completely forbidden in Islam. The prohibition of interest in Islam has implications on how to account for certain financial instruments such as bonds, discounted cash flows, notes, futures, and options. Gray, Owen, and Maunders (1988) argue that traditional accounting is also unable to avoid and control misappropriation of wealth and power and unsocial behavior of the dominating businessmen or companies. This led to products that are unique to Islamic financial institutions (e.g., "mudaraba," "musharaka," "murabaha," and "Ijara") with different rights and obligations associated with them. These products will be discussed later in this chapter.

Related to zakat is the historical cost principle, which is a key principle under IFRS. Under the historical cost principle, most assets are to be recorded on the balance sheet at their historical cost even if they have significantly increased in value over time. However, this principle is questionable from the Islamic point of view as it conflicts with the concepts of fairness and justice. In case of zakat determination, an overwhelming number of Muslim scholars recommended the use of current prices on the due date of zakat.

Another area of potential conflict between IFRS and Islamic accounting is the accrual basis of accounting. This has been the subject of discussion among Muslim scholars. Most scholars are in favor of applying cash basis accounting as a mode of practice to account for Islamic transactions. However, as economies in the Muslim world develop and new transactions emerge to facilitate the accounting for new transactions and the ever-increasing financial instruments, the nature of contracts and their underlying transactions have compelled examination of the cash accounting principle to ensure that accounting and financial reporting of these transactions reflect the true nature of the business and its underlying transactions.

One timing difference, which is rarely discussed, but leads to financial reporting difference, is that Islamic accounting is based on the Islamic calendar (lunar), while the solar or Gregorian calendar is used in conventional accounting. On average, there are 10 days less in the lunar year than in the solar year.

Although zakat functions like a tax, there are significant differences between the two. Zakat cannot be treated or regarded as another tax on wealth. The nature, objectives, and philosophy of zakat are different to that of tax. Generally speaking, all assets that are purchased for the purpose of resale would be subject to zakat. Raw materials and goods produced for sale are also subject to zakat. Assets used in business operations such as buildings, machinery, vehicles, accounts receivable, and prepaid expenses that are essential for the business are exempt from zakat. Other assets subject to zakat include gold, silver, cash, business assets and investments, animal livestock, and agricultural produce.

The example below illustrates the calculations of zakat:

Fixed assets

Property, plant, and equipment	400,000	Nonzakatable
Goodwill	350,000	Nonzakatable

Current assets

Inventory	250,000	Zakatable
Accounts receivables	100,000	Zakatable
Cash at bank	200,000	Zakatable
Petty cash	1,000	Zakatable
Prepaid expenses	5,000	Nonzakatable
Total zakatable assets	551,000	

Deductible liabilities

Creditors: amounts falling due within one lunar year

Accounts and other payables	10,000	Deductible
Loans and other borrowings	100,000	Deductible
Income tax	100,000	Deductible
Interest	10,000	Nondeductible
Total deductible liabilities	260,000	
Net zakatable assets	290,000	
Zakat due at 2.5 percent	7,250	

Adopted from National Zakat Foundation.

The Possibility of Agreement

Having listed possible conflicts between conventional and Islamic accounting, we suggest that these differences are not clear-cut or necessarily receive the support of all Muslim scholars. According to Maurer (2002), Islamic accounting standards are just replication of conventional accounting standards. It is just a mirage for Muslims and other professionals of Islamic banks that Islamic finance has separate accounting standards. Other scholars observed that the objectives of Islamic accounting standards are similar to conventional standards and did not pose any threat or challenge to conventional financing (Mirza and Baydoun 1999).

To explore the possibility of Islamic accounting standards being compliant with IFRS, the Accounting and Auditing Organization for Islamic Financial Institutions (AAOIFI) was established in Bahrain in 1990. Their task was to prepare accounting, auditing, governance, ethics and Sharia standards for Islamic financial institutions. This was followed by the Islamic Financial Services Board (IFSB) and the International Islamic Financial Market (IIFM), with the aim of providing standards for Islamic finance that are harmonized with global practices.

AAOIFI was established in accordance with the Agreement of Association, which was signed by Islamic financial institutions on February 26, 1990. It has members from more than 45 countries, including central banks, Islamic financial institutions, and other parties working in the financial industry and banking. It was created primarily to fill a gap for Islamic institutions that follow IFRS as a requirement but also need the Islamic standards to facilitate the calculation of zakat and provide guidance to Islamic banks on the ever-evolving financial instruments. AAOIFI has issued a Statement of Accounting Concepts to guide in the practice of accounting for Islamic financial institutions. The commission has obtained support for the application of the standards issued by it; these standards are applied today in Bahrain and the Dubai International Financial Centre, Jordan, Lebanon, Qatar, Sudan, and Syria.

AAOIFI has the following objectives:

- To develop accounting, auditing, governance, and ethical thought relating to the activities of Islamic financial institutions taking into consideration the international standards and practices which comply with Islamic Sharia rules.

- To disseminate the accounting, auditing, governance, and ethical thought relating to the activities of Islamic financial institutions and its application through training seminars.
- To harmonize the accounting policies and procedures adopted by Islamic financial institutions through the preparation and issuance of accounting standards and the interpretations of the same to the said institutions.
- To promote good ethical practices relating to Islamic financial institutions through the preparation and issuance of codes of ethics to these institutions.
- To approach the concerned regulatory bodies, Islamic financial institutions, other financial institutions that offer Islamic financial services, and accounting and auditing firms in order to implement the standards, as well as the statements and guidelines that are published by AAOIFI.
- To offer educational and training programs, including professional development programs on accounting, auditing, ethics, governance, Sharia, and other related areas, so as to promote knowledge on, and to encourage greater professionalism in, Islamic banking and finance. Training, examination, and certification shall be carried out by AAOIFI itself and/or in coordination with other institutions.
- To carry out other activities, including certification of compliance of AAOIFI's standards, to gain wider awareness and acceptance of AAOIFI's standards on accounting, auditing, ethics, governance, and Sharia.

The approach adopted by AAOIFI is not to develop the Islamic accounting concepts directly from the Islamic principles; instead the modern accounting concepts are tested against the Islamic values and Sharia principles. Those concepts that are not violating the Islamic principles will be accepted and those that are found to be in violation will be then either rejected or modified. To date, a total of 94 standards have been issued consisting of 54 Sharia standards, 26 accounting standards, 5 auditing standards, 2 codes of ethics, and 7 governance standards. The standards are published in two standards publications, namely

Sharia Standards publications, which contain all 54 Sharia standards, and Accounting, Auditing and Governance Standards publications, which contain all the other 40 standards on accounting, auditing, ethics, and governance. While many of the national standards, as well as those of AAOIFI, are closely aligned to IFRS, differences still remain, and practice can vary considerably.

A review of leading international Islamic financial institutions shows that a number of reporting frameworks are used across the industry. Although many use IFRS, some use partly converged IFRS-based standards, some use IFRS with additional requirements for Islamic banks, and others use standards exclusively for Islamic banks. Given the integration of the world economy and the internationalization of Islamic financial institutions, IFRS will play a major role. Even if a set of international Islamic financial accounting standards are used, they will have to be aligned with IFRS as much as possible, as can be seen in Table 4.1.

Table 4.1 Accounting standards applicable to Islamic banks by country

Country	Accounting standard(s)
Bahrain	AAOIFI and/or IFRS
Indonesia	Indonesian GAAP (AAOIFI)
Kuwait	IFRS and AAOIFI
Malaysia	Malaysian GAAP (with specific standards for financial institutions)
Pakistan	IFRS, with some local amendments for all banks
Qatar	AAOIFI
Saudi Arabia	IFRS (with additional requirements for all banks)
United Arab Emirates	IFRS (with additional requirements for all banks)

Source: Adopted from a KPMG study "Harmonizing Financial Reporting of Islamic Finance," 2010.

AAOIFI is a not-for-profit organization. As such, it does not possess the power of enforcement of implementation of its standards. It would not be an easy task for AAOIFI to have all Islamic countries adhere to its standards, because of existing different legislations and regulatory requirements (Ehsan, Saeed, Shahzad, and Iqbal 2018). Many standard-setter regulators do not share AAOIFI's views on accounting or what constitutes compliance with Sharia.

PWC (2010) argues that any transaction can be accounted for and reported within IFRS financial statements. In those cases where there are no specific IFRS requirements, any treatment that does not conflict with the framework may be adopted. However, where alternatives are possible, IFRS requires that their relevance and reliability are assessed to select the most appropriate option. In turn, any Islamic finance transaction can be analyzed to determine how it should be accounted for under IFRS where principles can invariably be applied without resorting to conflicting approaches. To the extent that IFRS determines presentation and disclosure, then IFRS should also be applied to this aspect of Islamic finance transactions. However, the IFRS disclosure framework does not cover all the needs of stakeholders of Islamic finance institutions, as is the case of zakat, for example. Therefore, it would be helpful if there was additional guidance for IFRS preparers in two specific areas: (1) guidance on the application of IFRS when accounting for Islamic finance instruments and (2) guidance regarding the additional disclosures that should be made for the benefit of stakeholders seeking information on Sharia compliance.

Major efforts are already in place to reconcile IFRS to Islamic finance, and to bring Islamic finance more clearly within the overall IFRS framework, the Asian Oceanian Standard Setters Group has set up a Working Group to liaise with the IASB on the application of IFRS to Islamic finance. According to the group's survey conducted in 2015, 46 percent of the Islamic financial institutions asserted compliance with either IFRS or IFRS as adopted by a specific jurisdiction, while 18 percent asserted compliance with AAOIFI FAS. Significantly, 34 percent asserted compliance with local GAAP.

Accounting Principles in Islam

Islamic accounting does not require specific form that followers should implement. However, the focus is that the form followed must meet the most important basic principles of Islam. These are accountability, justice, and truth. Truthful and relevant disclosure of information is of paramount importance in Islam. The guidance on how to achieve these aims is sometimes broader than one finds in international accounting standards. For example, recording activities and transactions is explicitly mentioned in the *Qur'an*: "Believers, when you contract a debt for a fixed period, put it in writing. Let a scribe write it down fairly . . . and let the debtor dictate, not diminishing the sum he owes . . ." (S2:282).

Apart from this example, most of the guidance on principles are not dissimilar to the standards issued by the IASB. For example, associated with full disclosure is the concept of relevance. In an Islamic context, disclosure of all facts is required. The public has the right to know the effects of an organization's operations on its well-being and to be advised within the requirements of Sharia as to how this has been achieved. As for reliability, 19 verses in the *Qur'an* explicitly emphasize reliability of matter (Askary and Clarke 1997). As with every other aspect of Islamic secular life, reliability extends into the area of accounting. If published financial information is unreliable, many followers will be unable to fulfill their religious responsibilities as they will be unable to assess their capacity to assist the disadvantaged, or their capacity to pay zakat.

The Main Accounting Concepts and Assumption in Islamic Accounting

Entity Concept:
The entity concept states that the firm and its owners are separate entities. Therefore, the owners (with limited liability) are not liable for the liabilities of the firms. Islamic Sharia disagrees with the concept because the owners are not liable for the company's debt at the time of bankruptcy— but have the rights to residual profits which is unlawful and similar to gambling (Napier 2007). However, in Islamic accounting, if the owners become bankrupt, then the liabilities may be distributed to their successors or legal inheritors. The entity concept has been a matter of debate by Muslim scholars and standard setters. AAOIFI, however, has examined the entity concept. It was found that the accounting entity concept, that is, the entity created as a separate unit of accountability, is acceptable in Islam as it resembles the widely practiced trust foundation (waqf) and Islamic Treasury (Baitul Maal) in Muslim traditions.

Going Concern:

Going concern is an assumption of the business or the entity as a going concern or to continue for foreseeable future unless there is a significant evidence to the contrary. Islamic scholars have different views on the assumption of going concern. Some view this assumption as a direct contradiction to the teaching of Sharia; others view it as an important assumption to Islamic institution to conduct business. The going concern concept is applicable to most Islamic financial contracts especially for Islamic banking contracts such as musharaka and mudaraba. An assumption has be made that the contract shall continue for the foreseeable future until one or all of the parties involved decide to terminate such contracts. This assumption is important especially for Islamic banks as it assumes, based on financial position and performance, the continuity of the bank's activities in the future including its investment activities.

Accounting Period:

This is one of the few concepts that Islamic and traditional accounting agree. The main point behind this agreement is the calculation and payment of zakat, which is paid once a year; the *Qur'an* specifically mentions that the wealth must be owned for at least one year to qualify for the payment of zakat. The financial statements representing the financial performance and financial position of the business are periodically disclosed based on this concept. In Islamic points of view, this concept may be accepted based on the ground that zakat is paid annually and the condition for applicability of zakat is holding of assets for one year. Accounting statements should be prepared for a particular period, showing the amounts on which zakat would be levied (Adnan and Gaffikin 1997).

The periodicity concept for an Islamic financial institution means the life of the institution can be broken into reporting periods to prepare financial reports to the interested parties and stakeholders. This will assist the users to periodically evaluate the institution's financial performance and position. In addition, the periodic preparation of the financial statements will be useful to determine the financial obligations and the financial rights of the bank and other interested parties.

Money Measurement:

The money measurement concept states that the events recorded in accounting must be measurable in terms of money to facilitate the recording of various events and transactions. But those events that cannot be expressed in terms of money are not recorded. One of the weaknesses of this concept is that the purchasing power of money is unstable especially in inflationary environment and this affects future financial rights and obligations. Therefore, the role of money as a standard of measure is questioned by different Islamic scholars. Ahmed (1990) stated that using money as a unit of measurement is questionable from Islamic perspective in an inflationary situation and hence money is unable to serve as a just and honest unit of account. However, most of the scholars argue that because of unavailability of any suitable standard, money can be taken as a standard of expressing diverse objects in a common denominator (Napier 2007). In an interest-free economy, money may be used in recording transactions without any question. Islamic accounting records and prepares reports relating to some transactions, which may not be possible to measure in terms of money (e.g., environmental damages/ degradation by the firm).

Historical Cost:

According to this concept, the asset acquired should be recorded and stated in the financial statements at its cost because the cost amount is objective and verifiable. But, for the calculation of zakat, the assets are required to be recorded at current market value. This is because the real (just and fair) picture of the organizations cannot be revealed with historical cost, which can be misleading and outdated. The cost concept for valuation corrupts the principle of disclosing the truth to the interested users (Al-Qur'an 2:42). However, if current value is used, then any profit or loss resulting from the revaluation may be distributed among the stockholders before it is earned, and this represents sharp contradictions with Islamic values. Another potential problem with using market values is that these values are subjective and cannot be verified.

Due to the above potential problems, most Muslim scholars suggest adopting the cost principle with modification when calculating zakat. Mirza and Baydoun (2000) propose using both valuation methods in

Islamic accounting, that is, the contractual transactions with other parties should be based on cost, and zakat calculation (assets valuation) should be based on current market value. AAOIFI explained that the calculation of zakat requires the calculation of assets and liabilities through fair value (cash equivalent value) to be used as the basis for the imposition of zakat. It indicates that the more accurate measurement of assets using fair value is the equivalent cash value of the Islamic perspective, so that the measurement of fair value does not provide uncertainty about whether the current price figure relates to the current condition of the assets and liabilities.

Conservatism:

This concept requires company accounts to be prepared with caution and high degrees of verification. All probable losses are recorded when they are discovered, while gains can only be registered when they are fully realized. The basis of the concept is to ignore possible future profits but account for possible losses if they meet the conditions of being probable and can be measured reliably. In short, this concept states that if accountants have reasonable choice, they should record assets and revenues at lower figures and liabilities and expenses at higher figures. It acts as a constraint to the presentation of relevant and reliable data (Belkaoui 2000). This concept is in conflict with the *Qur'an* because it would lead to understatement of assets, which is the basis of Zakat calculation. Ahmed (1990) stated that though this concept contradicts *with* Islamic principles, it restricts overoptimistic valuations and distribution of unearned profit. The *Qur'an* instructs Muslims to choose and follow medium paths avoiding the extremes (Al-Qur'an, 25:67 and 17:29).

Accounting for Interest

Islamic banking is a system of banking that is based on the principles of Sharia law. Sharia law prohibits the receipt and payment of interest, known as "riba." It also prohibits undertaking excessive uncertainty, gambling, and short sales or financing activities that it considers harmful to society. The fundamental concept of Islamic banking is that money itself has no intrinsic value; it is simply a medium of exchange. Interest is prohibited in Islam as it appears explicitly in the holy *Qur'an*. There is consensus among all Islamic scholars regarding the prohibition of interest. Ali (1992) in his commentary on the holy *Qur'an* mentioned that interest is condemned and prohibited in the strongest possible terms. So, there can be no question about the prohibition.

Interest is the predetermined fixed charge on borrowing or investing money but any transactions relating to interest (in any form) is strictly prohibited by Islamic Sharia. Hence, Islamic organizations (banks) use alternative modes of borrowings/investments to meet their needs of financing. These alternatives are discussed below:

(a) *Mudaraba (trust financing)*:

Mudaraba is a business contract between one party which brings capital (usually the bank) and an entrepreneur; any profit generated from the capital is shared between the entrepreneur and the bank according to mutually agreed profit-sharing ratio. Any financial losses, however, are borne by the bank provided that such losses are not due to the entrepreneur's misconduct, negligence, or breach of specified terms, and the borrower receives no reward for his effort. Kahf (1978) defines mudaraba as an Islamic mechanism for introducing monetary assets into production activity by transforming them into real factors of production because of a joint action between the owner of the assets and the entrepreneur. In a typical mudaraba contract, the bank acts as a partner, providing cash to the borrower and sharing in the net profits and net losses of the business (Haqiqi and Pomeranz 1987). The loan is for an undetermined period, although the contract may be rescinded by either party.

(b) *Murabaha (cost-plus trade financing)*:

The purpose of *murabaha* is to finance a purchase without involving interest payments and it has come to be the most prevalent or "default" type of Islamic finance. The contracts are typically used if the client wants to purchase equipment or goods. The bank will purchase these items and then sell them to the customer at cost plus a reasonable profit. From an accounting viewpoint, the bank uses cost of goods sold as an intermediary account (i.e., debit the cost of goods sold when the asset is purchased, and credit the account when the asset is sold to the customer). The other side of the transaction will be reflected in the bank's balance sheet as an investment.

(c) *Musharaka (participation financing)*:

Musharaka is a joint partnership arrangement in Islamic finance in which profits and losses are shared. The profit will be shared between the two parties based on mutually agreed-upon ratio (cannot be the ratio of capital contributed). Losses, however, are usually shared based on the capital contributed by each partner. This method is frequently used to finance large purchases, for example, the purchase of property and real estate, providing credit, investment projects, and, real estate deals. Every party that puts up capital is entitled to a say in the property's management. When musharaka is employed to finance large purchases, banks usually lend by using floating-rate interest loans pegged to a company's rate of return. That "peg" serves as a lending partner's profit. In case of a default, both the buyer and the lender get a share of the proceeds from the sale of the property on a pro rata basis. This differs from more traditional lending structures in which the lender alone benefits from any property sale following foreclosure.

Musharaka is considered an asset in the balance sheet; once the funds are available to other partners, the bank will reflect this as "musharaka financing" in its balance sheet. If the bank provides nonmonetary assets, these assets are valued at fair market value and revalued at the end of each year. Any gains or losses from the valuation is shown in the income statement.

(d) *Ijara (rental/lease financing)*:

Ijara, sometimes referred to as halal mortgage, is an agreement whereby the lessor conveys the right to use a specified asset to the lessee for an agreed-upon period of time in return of a fair rent. In Ijara financing, a bank purchases fixed assets and allows the clients to use in return for rental income. A typical example can be finance lease (a long-time lease where the lessee gets the ownership of the asset) or an operating lease (a short-time lease where the lessor retains the ownership of the asset). Sharia permits Ijara contracts so long as they are not tied to interest rate. The lessee's total rental payable or the bank's total rental income varies according to changes in the rate of return of the bank. In case of finance lease, lease receivable, less the profit margin, which is not received, should be recorded as fixed assets in the balance sheet, and with an operating lease—the lease—assets should be recorded as fixed assets in the balance sheet of the lessor and depreciation for these assets is provided periodically (Hamat 1994).

The following example illustrates how Ijara works:

i. A person (the buyer) chooses a property and pays the required down payment. The down payment is anywhere between 3.5 and 20 percent. This could be higher if the person chooses a higher one. The title of the property will be held by an independent trust. Then the trust leases the property to the buyer (the lessee) for up to 30 years for a monthly rent to be paid to the trust. At the end of the lease period, the title is transferred to the lessee for a nominal fee (typically $1.00).

ii. Should the personal situation for the lessee change and he or she has a need to sell the house, the trust is informed of this need and an arrangement is made to sell the house. If there is a profit, the lessee keeps 100 percent of the profit. If there is a loss, the lessee bears the first loss.

iii. Even though the "Lease to Purchase" program was specifically designed to meet the religious obligations of Muslims, it is made available to all qualified people in the United States and Canada that are interested in a Sharia-Compliant Financing Product.

(e) *Takaful*:

Takaful is a type of Islamic insurance wherein members contribute money into a pool system to guarantee each other against loss or damage. Takaful-branded insurance is based on Sharia or Islamic religious law, which explains how individuals are responsible to cooperate and protect one another. Starting from the 1970s, and increasingly in the 1990s, Islamic countries and others with a significant Muslim population have encouraged the provision of financial services, including insurance, under Islamic principles. As a result, a number of Islamic insurance companies, called takaful insurers, have been established to provide Muslim individuals and businesses with insurance coverage both in the life and in the nonlife sectors (Al-Amri and Hossain 2015). The main ideology of takaful is to bear the other person's burden and there is no profit in this system. Some of the important principles of takaful are as follows:

i. For the common good, the policy holders will corporate with each other.

ii. The contribution of the policy holders is considered donations.

iii. To help those who need assistance, all their policy holders will pay their share.

iv. The liabilities are shared according to the pooling system of the community and losses are divided.

v. According to compensation and subscription, there is no uncertainty because of the differences between takaful and conventional insurance contracts; several takaful providers argue that some of the concepts in IFRS 4 for insurers may not be appropriate. PWC (2010) states that "while the operational models may differ, the economic substance of risk sharing, which is the basis of IFRS 4, is still appropriate for takaful business."

Conclusions

The rapid growth of the Muslim population worldwide (5 percent in Europe, 4.7 percent in Canada, 1 percent in the United States of the total population) necessitated the creation of Islamic institutions (namely banks) in those countries. One of the most important attractions of these institutions is that they adhere to Islamic laws. From an accounting viewpoint, this poses a challenge to these institutions since the countries where they are located (with the notable exception of the United States) follow IFRS. As discussed in the chapter, IFRS is not fully compatible with Islamic law. To address the needs of these institutions, AAOIFI was created in 1990 as a standards setter for Islamic institutions. Differences between AAOIFI and IFRS exist and will continue to exist because of the differences in structural objectives.

In reality, most of these institutions follow IFRS and prepare their financial statements accordingly. Most of them, however, prepare two sets of financial statements to meet the regulations of the countries in which they are located and to accommodate the need of their customer base.

Given the flexibility of IFRS, we anticipate that more and more Islamic transactions will be covered under IFRS, starting with those transactions that are unique to the Muslim religions and are not currently addressed.

CHAPTER 5

The Future of Corporate Reporting

Introduction

In this final chapter, we focus less on the financial information given by companies to shareholders, than the developments that are changing the nature of the information being provided by companies to a wider audience. One assumption that has influenced the provision of information by companies is that they are responsible to and reporting to shareholders who seek a financial return from any investment they have made. This is a narrow view of the role of a company in present times. As well as paying dividends to shareholders, companies also create employment, provide goods and services, pay taxes to the government, and, in some respects, influence the way we live. Given that wide spread of connections it is not surprising that the activities and actions of companies are of interest to many people. Frequently, that interest is not focused simply on the dividends paid and the current price of shares in the market, but on a range of issues.

In the first section, we describe the move from concentrating on financial reporting to shareholders only to a broader view of the various interests in corporate activities and the information that may satisfy those interests. This is followed by a section that looks at the specific pressures and decisions that led to changes in corporate reporting. For this section, we focus on the sources of control and influence that have led to the changes. We then consider the changes in the United Kingdom, the United States, and Islamic countries. One of the greatest changes is that many counties no longer set their own financial reporting standards but there are international regulations and we consider the developments at the international level in detail. In the final section, we discuss the impact of technology on corporate reporting with particular emphasis on eXtensible Business Reporting Language (XBRL).

Spreading the Word (What Word?)

After the ravages of the Second World War the 1950s showed an increase in business activity, which had an impact on all our lives. There was more work and more money. After much dispute and debate in the United States, it was announced that a phased increase in the minimum wage would bring everyone up to the established minimum rates by December 1965. It was also claimed that there would be more profits for the shareholders. In the 1960s, retail prices in the United Kingdom increased. However, earnings had increased more and it is also claimed that rates of pay for male manual workers improved greatly.

This general increase in wealth of companies and employees raised the question of the purpose of financial reports issued by companies. May (1943) had argued that company financial reports were important as a guide for deciding whether to buy, hold, or sell securities. He argued that it was essential for investors to receive this information. This was not the final answer to a debate, which was only beginning. Later work by Sprouse and Moonitz (1961) stimulated discussions in the United States and the United Kingdom and, in 1973, the Financial Accounting Standards Board (FASB) in the United States commenced a search for a conceptual framework designed to resolve many unanswered questions. In the draft issued in 1978, it was stated that financial information should provide information that is useful to present and potential investors and creditors and other users in making rational investment, credit, and similar decisions.

This claim from an authoritative body deflected the attention on only shareholders, and, by a discussion paper issued by the Accounting Standards Steering Committee (ASSC), identified seven user groups including employees and equity investors. This expansion of interests theme was strengthened by Macve (1981) who argued that the objective of financial reporting was to aid those who wish to check on the honesty and stewardship of management, to confirm the compliance with company law, and to check the reasonableness of the dividend being declared. The U.S. views were accompanied by researches and papers in the United Kingdom considering the objective of financial reports.

Although much of the interest was on the provision of financial information to shareholders, in the 1950s several companies were giving financial information to employees. In the United Kingdom, in 1948, The Metal Box company produced a full-color booklet for employees written by Sir Robert Barlow, the company's chairman. It was issued at the same time as the annual company accounts. The British Institute of Management in 1957 conducted a survey of 89 companies that were already giving financial information to employees. Of these companies 59 were giving the same annual report to employees as issued to all shareholders. There was a substantial growth in this practice with larger- and medium-sized companies. The reason for this greater use of reports to employees was easy to explain. The larger companies were already making their financial reports publicly available so there were no constraints of confidentiality and the extended print run of the reports would be negligible.

There were several reasons companies adopted the practice. Some considered that employees should not be denied at least as much information as shareholders whose connection with the company may be very short and only financial. Another reason was that the human school of management theory that improved employee communications led to better employee relations. There was also the "band wagon" effect where companies adopted the practice because other companies were doing it.

The nature of the information given to employees over the years was expanded. The BIM survey in 1957 demonstrated a wide range of information provided to employees at that time. Of the 89 large companies 70 percent gave a forecast of trading position, 64 percent the profit and loss account, and 52 percent the balance sheet. A later study by Marsh and Hussey (1979) of 302 employee reports—the term frequently used to identify the documents—found that 77 percent of the documents showed financial highlights, 41 percent a value-added statement, 39 percent a balance sheet, and 25 percent a profit and loss account. Over the years the types of information disclosed varied but it was argued that companies were supplying information which best meets the providers' convenience rather the user's needs (Trade Union Research Unit 1981).

Sources of Control and Influence

All countries have laws that regulate the operations of companies and determine the financial information which should be given to shareholders. Initially, it was usually the professional accounting bodies that set out the detailed requirements and issued guidelines, briefing notes, and other documents to their members to assist them in conducting their work. This system, however, was not sufficiently robust to ensure that the published financial statements provided information that gave a faithful representation of the activities of the entity.

The move to a more formal process with standard setters normally being independent of the professional accounting bodies and, in most countries, having some form of legal authority did much to improve the quality of financial statements. It was in the 1970s that in various countries standard setting bodies and committees were established and the term *accounting standards* came into widespread use. The ASSC in the United Kingdom was established in 1970. The U.S. FASB succeeded the Accounting Principles Board (APB) on July 1, 1973, two days after the IASC was formed. Some countries were late in their approach and the Malaysian Accounting Standards Board (MASB) was not formed until 1997.

Every country has its own regulations, usually complex, for the various types of companies operating in its borders. Certainly, the accounting bodies set a platform but it was the regulatory framework within a country that established the nature and form of disclosure of information by companies. With different types of companies, regulatory methods, and existing regulatory practices, countries developed their own requirements for the disclosure of information by companies and at different times.

In this section, we explain the development of regulations and we concentrate on two countries, the United Kingdom and the United States that have been active in regulations. We also review the position in Islamic countries that add a very different approach. At one time our interest would be solely on financial information but, in most regimes, corporate reporting is now much wider and we consider the position in the United Kingdom, the United States, and Islamic accounting. If we are considering the financial statements issued by a company, understanding the source of the regulations is essential. Some countries such as the United States issue their own accounting standards. Other countries such as the United Kingdom apply international accounting standards (IASs) and these are discussed in detail in the next section.

The United Kingdom

The United Kingdom applies the accounting standards issued by the International Accounting Standards Board (IASB). The role of the Financial Reporting Council (FRC) in the United Kingdom is for financial accounting and reporting by all types of limited liability companies. However, it is not the responsibility of the FRC to issue standards that apply to financial statements. These are given in Companies Acts issued by the UK government, the latest being the Companies Act 2006. The directors of a company are responsible for the accuracy of the financial statements. The Companies Act includes many proclamations and requirements of its own, and a brief review of these is given in Anders (2015). It also establishes the United Kingdom's Corporate Governance and Stewardship Codes and has the overall objective of promoting transparency and integrity in business. The FRC regulates auditors, accountants, and actuaries and is responsible for the United Kingdom's Corporate Governance and Stewardship Codes, to those who rely on company reports, and for audit and high-quality risk management.

In its Corporate Reporting Review work, the FRC ensures that the provision of financial information by public and large private companies complies with relevant reporting requirements. The FRC reviews the directors' reports and accounts of public and large private companies for compliance with the law. It also keeps under review interim reports of all listed issuers and annual reports of certain other noncorporate listed entities. The FRC investigates cases where it appears that the legal requirements have not been followed. Usually this is where there is, or may be, a question of whether the directors' report or accounts complies with the requirements of the Companies Act 2006.

In July 2018, the FRC published its Corporate Governance Code which applies to accounting periods beginning on or after January 1, 2019 (Financial Reporting Council 2018). The code places greater emphasis on relationships between companies, shareholders, and stakeholders. It also promotes the importance of establishing a corporate culture that is aligned with the company purpose and business strategy. It promotes integrity and values diversity. All companies with a premium listing of equity shares in the United Kingdom are required under the listing rules of the stock exchange to report in their annual report and accounts how they have applied the code. Although the code does not have international authority, a requirement by the FRC is that companies with shares listed on the UK Stock Exchange or AIM (Alternative Investment Market) and issuing consolidated financial statements must comply with the code.

On March 11, 2019, it was announced that the FRC would be replaced with a new regulator called the Audit, Reporting and Governance Authority (ARGA), which will have stronger statutory powers (Business Energy and Industrial Strategy (BEIS) 2019). The new regulator

- Is a statutory body with powers such as those to make direct changes to accounts rather than apply to court to do so
- Has strategic direction and duties to protect the interests of customers and the public by setting high standards of statutory audit, corporate reporting, and corporate governance and by holding companies and professional advisors to account
- Regulates the biggest audit firms directly (rather than those being delegated)
- Has a new, diverse board and strong leadership to change the culture and rebuild respect of those it regulates

The new authority's responsibility is much broader than only ensuring the application of IASs. It will focus on the entire corporate report. We do not envisage that this will directly impact on the work of the IASB but it should strengthen the requirement for United Kingdom to comply completely with international standards. It is not possible to forecast how the actions of the new authority in the United Kingdom may impact on other countries. It has been suggested that the new body would reduce the dominance of the Big Four audit firms PwC, Deloitte, EY, and KPMG that audit the overwhelming majority of FTSE 350 listed businesses.

ARGA will be governed by a simplified board with strengthened oversight, and nonexecutive members including the chair will be public appointments. The regulator will be accountable to parliament, with strategic direction from the government. It will also strengthen its corporate reporting review function and its oversight of audit committees and will enforce the corporate reporting duties of directors. The enforcement powers of ARGA will apply to breaches by directors of the existing statutory duties relating to corporate reporting and company audits. These duties include, among other matters, the duty to keep adequate accounting records and the duty to approve accounts only if they give a true and fair view which means that it is free from material misstatements and faithfully represents the financial performance and positioning of an entity.

The United States

The United States provides an example of a country that does not use IASs and maintains its own regulations. The accounting standard setter in the United States is the Securities and Exchange Commission (SEC), which is a large independent agency of the United States federal government. The SEC was created in 1934 after the Wall Street Crash and was established to protect investors. It achieves this by maintaining orderly and efficient markets; assisting capital formation, and enforcing the law against market manipulation.

The SEC adopted proposed disclosure amendments in 1973 which required companies to disclose environmental information. This initiative was followed in 1975 by the SEC court-ordered hearings on "Disclosure of Environmental and Other Socially Significant Matters." This resulted in disclosure rules pertaining to capital expenditure for environmental compliance purposes.

Corporate social responsibility (CSR) has been under greater scrutiny recently as more companies realize that their environmental efforts, ethical labor practices, and corporate governance are of increasing concern to various stakeholders and therefore affect business success. According to a KPMG (2011) corporate sustainability report, more firms are measuring and reporting sustainability performance, and there is a greater need for consistent measurement and analysis of sustainability metrics for disclosure purposes. Although sustainability reporting is not required in the United States, many companies issue separate annual sustainability reports recognizing the importance of keeping their various stakeholders informed of initiatives and policies to mitigate social risks. These companies often use the Global Initiative Reporting guidelines to prepare sustainability reports; these reports are one facet considered in determining a company's Bloomberg Environmental–Social–Governance (ESG) disclosure score.

Bloomberg ESG scores apply a multidimensional construct, based on about 120 quantitative and qualitative measures, to rate companies on their environmental ("E"), social ("S"), and governance ("G") policies and practices. To construct the scores, publicly available data, annual and sustainability reports, direct communication, press releases, third-party research, and news items are used. The three ESG scores each ranging from 0 indicating no disclosure to 100 demonstrating complete disclosure are then combined into a single score (ranging from 0 to 100) using a proprietary method. ESG scores and ratings of companies are updated and include such subjects as greenhouse gas (GHG) emissions, electricity usage, waste discarded, ISO 14000 environmental certification, policies against child labor, antibribery ethics policies, size of the board of directors, percentage of women on the board of directors, and average age of board members. The more information disclosed by the company, the higher the disclosure score but it is not measuring performance, but the level of commitment to transparency and accountability. The data set offers ESG metrics and disclosure scores for more than 11,500 companies in 80+ countries. This includes as-reported data and derived rations as well as sector- and country-specific data points. Historical data since 2006 are available, and the link is www.bloomberg.com/professional/ dataset/global-environmental-social-governance-data/.

The Bloomberg data scores were used in a study by Tamimi and Sebastianelli (2017). Data were retrieved from Bloomberg using the financial analysis environmental, social, and governance function for the companies comprising the S&P 500. Some of the collected data are measured on a ratio scale (e.g., water usage, waste discarded, etc.), while other data are measured qualitatively on a "yes" or "no" basis (e.g., whether the company has a policy on child labor or if executive compensation is linked to ESG scores). The researchers used nonparametric methods for analyzing data because the ESG metrics are qualitative, and disclosure scores (composite as well as those for each of the three dimensions) are skewed. The researchers concluded that S&P 500 companies are most transparent regarding governance disclosures (likely resulting from the SEC's mandate that requires public companies to disclose data related to financial and governance metrics), but that significant deficiencies exist with respect to disclosing information on environmental and social practices. However, ESG disclosures attract growing interest as demonstrated by the increasing number of customers using Bloomberg ESG data, with the usage increasing from 1,545 in 2009 to 12,078 in 2015 (www.bloomberg.com/bcause/customers-using-esg-data). We discuss this interest at the international level in a later section as the information available suggests the need for international corporate social reporting.

As standard setters, the FASB cannot claim unique characteristics that are not shared by other standard setters. It is well resourced and has extremely knowledgeable people working for it—as do other organizations, but possibly with not so much resourcing. However, it can be argued that other countries have followed U.S. GAAP for reasons other than the excellence of the standards.

First, there was the requirement for many years that foreign companies wishing to list in the United States had to comply with U.S. GAAP. Although that requirement has changed, several foreign companies already listed have continued to comply rather than the effort of changing their accounting procedures to comply with IFRSs.

Second, the size of the U.S. capital markets has historically attracted companies and investors. That position has weakened during some periods. This observation is not meant to minimize the strength of the U.S. markets, but to note that the international competition is becoming stronger.

Third, the United States has many international companies and extensive business involvement with several countries. The U.S. GAAP had, therefore, become the lingua franca of accounting in some regimes. What the United States has been able to offer, which is missing in some countries, is strong compliance and enforcement procedures. Nearly every research study that examines the application of IFRS emphasizes that the extent of compliance is not due to the defects of the standards but due to the lack of rigorous enforcement of the standards in some jurisdictions. Countries can copy the requirements of U.S. GAAP or IFRS, but this does not mean that domestic financial statements are truly convergent with IFRS.

There are also barriers within a country, not only the United States.

A study of four countries identified three dominant factors that are barriers to accounting convergence. These are:

1. The nature of business ownership and the financial system
2. Culture
3. The level of accounting education and the experience of professional accountants

We discussed such factors in earlier chapters, but the above findings highlight the fact that it is not necessarily the regulations set by the standard setters that are the issue, but the environment in which they are being applied. As long as the standards are considered to be of high quality, it does not matter whether the FASB or the IASB sets them; the crucial ingredient is the structure within a country that ensures organizational compliance.

Islamic Accounting

Although the roots of Islamic accounting date back to the 17th and the 18th centuries, it only came to the forefront in the last 30 years. The major factor in the development of the Islamic accounting standards was the wide-spreading of Islamic financial institutions. It is common nowadays to find Islamic financial institutions in countries like the United States, United Kingdom, Canada, and Australia.

These developments require accounting standards to be adopted to govern the setting up of these institutions and contributing to the objective of high accounting quality and comparability as suggested by Barth *et al.* (2012). The introduction of IFRS in 1970s and their increased popularity gave a boost to Islamic accounting standards. PWC (2010) notes that "The principles-based nature of IFRS makes it possible to recognize, measure and disclose the economic substance of Islamic finance without compromising Sharia principles." The general trend in most Muslim countries is to adopt IFRS principles wherever possible. In areas of conflict, Islamic accounting principles can be developed.

International Accounting

In the latter half of the 20th century, there were some highly publicized examples of very profitable companies in Europe that wanted to list their shares on the New York Stock Exchange (NYSE). In order to do so, the profitable company had to redraft those financial statements in accordance to U.S. GAAP. In some instances, the previously declared profit for a financial year turned into a loss. Thus, a conceptual inconsistency exists as the activities of a particular company in a specific financial period can show either a profit or loss depending on which national accounting regime applies.

Possibly the most famous case is that of Daimler Benz AG, a German company that wished to list its shares on the U.S. Stock Exchange in the early 1990s. To do so it had to reconcile the profit it had shown for 1993 using German GAAP with what the profit would have been if it had used U.S. GAAP. The net income, or profit, the company had reported in its German financial statements, was DM 615 million. After the company had made all the adjustments to comply with U.S. GAAP, the reported net income turned to a net loss of DM 1,839 million. Such a huge difference demonstrated the accounting at the international level did not make sense. It is confusing to investors and others to say that Daimler Benz made either a good profit or massive loss depending on which country's regulations were used.

Although Daimler Benz highlighted the problem, the issue of significant differences in national accounting standards had been recognized at an early stage. In 1973, national accountancy bodies from Australia, Canada, France, Germany, Mexico, the Netherlands, the United Kingdom and Ireland, and the United States established the International Accounting Standards Committee (IASC). The objectives of the IASC were:

- To formulate and publish, in the public interest, accounting standards to be observed in the presentation of financial

statements and to promote their worldwide acceptance
and observance

- To work generally for the improvement and harmonization of
regulations, accounting standards, and procedures relating to
the presentation of financial statements

These objectives were extremely ambitious for an organization that
was resourced very modestly and had no enforcement powers. The IASC
intended to achieve these objectives by:

- Ensuring that published financial statements comply with
IASs in all material respect
- Persuading governments and standard setting bodies that
published financial statements to comply with IASs
- Persuading authorities controlling securities markets and the
industrial and business community that published financial
statements to comply with IASs

One major factor in promoting the role of the IASC was the reaction
of the emerging economies. Many were attempting to establish themselves
in international trade or to move away from command economies. The
IASC offered a quick and viable way for establishing an appropriate
they carried none of the possible political implications from adopting
the standards of one particular country. A second factor assisting the
IASC was the increased encouragement from several organizations and
countries to pursue the goal of international harmonization more rapidly
and effectively.

In 1992, the three standard setting bodies of Canada, the United
Kingdom, and the United States met to discuss some of the accounting
issues confronting them. A major problem was the proper treatment for
provisions and the three countries agreed to work jointly in seeking a
solution. Australia later joined the working group, as did New Zealand.
This was the start of the G4 + 1 and an invitation was given to the IASC
(the +1) to join them. The reason for this inclusion was mainly political,
as the original English-speaking countries did not wish to be criticized for
attempting to set an international accounting agenda unilaterally. G4 + 1

addressed a number of major accounting issues from a strong conceptual basis and also became involved with discussions on the structure and
effectiveness of IASC. In the proposals that the group made on the future
of the IASC, it appeared to many critics that the G4 + 1 would have
increasing power over IASs. The group denied that this was their intent
but there is no doubt of their influence in the way the IAS setting has
been established. In January 2001, it was agreed that the G4 + 1 group
would disband as the IASB was ready taking over from IASC. The G4 + 1
group cancelled its proposed future activities and submitted its current
work to the IASB as potential future projects.

The present structure for IASs consists of the IFRS Foundation and
the IASB. The foundation is a not-for-profit international organization
responsible for developing IFRS standards. The IASB is an independent
group of experts and its objectives are:

- To develop, in the public interest, a single set of high-quality,
  understandable, and enforceable global accounting standards
- To help participants in the world's capital markets and other
  users make economic decisions by having access to
  high-quality, transparent, and comparable information
- To promote the use and vigorous application of those standards
- To bring about convergence of national accounting standards
  and IASs to high-quality solutions

It can be claimed that the IFRS has been a success, and on its website it claims that 166 jurisdictions and their websites identify the IFRS
requirements relevant to different jurisdictions.

Technology

Internet Reporting

The use of the Internet for corporate reporting by companies has grown
substantially over recent years and provides users with easy access to corporate information. It allows companies to communicate text, graphics,
sound, and video. Before 1995, there was very little use of the technology
for disseminating financial information. In 1996, the practice developed

and then grew rapidly. Research by Craven and Marston (1999) examined the largest 200 companies as listed by market capitalization in the *Financial Times*, January 22, 1998, and Table 5.1 shows the types of disclosures.

The researchers identified two independent variables: company size and industry type. There were four size variables: turnover, number of

Table 5.1 Summary of financial reporting on the Internet by the sample of top UK companies, 1998

Financial disclosure	Number	Percentage
Detailed annual report	67	32.5
Parts or summaries of annual report	42	20.4
Website but no financial information	44	21.3
No website	52	25.2
Unclear/ambiguous	1	0.5
Total	206	100

employees, total assets employed, and average market value. There were six different industrial categories. The researchers conducted statistical analysis and we summarize the main findings:

- For each one of the four size variables, companies with a website had a median size about twice as large compared to companies without a website.
- There were positive associations between the size variables and the extent of financial disclosure on the Internet.
- There was no relationship between industry type and the extent of financial disclosure on the Internet based on the sample of 206 large companies.

The above study was conducted over 20 years ago, and the use of the Internet for corporate reporting has expanded substantially. Commercial usage of the Internet continues to expand for product/service marketing, and for corporate reporting also, it has grown in usage. The IFRS Foundation believes that the structured electronic reporting of IFRS financial statements assists its own mission statement in the following ways:

Assists transparency: increases accessibility of information for all market participants

Assists accountability: structured electronic data supports market enforcement of IFRS by regulators

Assists efficiency: accessible data may reduce costs to process IFRS information allowing users to focus on analysis

Source: *www.ifrs.org/XBRL/Pages/XBRL.aspx*

Although there have been several studies that have focused on corporate disclosures on the Internet, one by Rowbottom, Allam, and Lymer (2005) focused on the corporate information Internet users seek. The study measured online information using activity logs from the webserver as this fulfills user requests for information over the Internet. They gathered data from a UK FTSE 100 company. The researchers carefully explain the limitations of the methodology and the issues in interpretation of the results. The web log analyses do not provide absolute levels of online information usage. They measure what information is demanded online. They do not indicate whether the information has been used or read. They provide a proxy measure of online IR information usage and are not an appropriate proxy for general IR information usage. Having given those disclaimers, we summarize some of the findings most relevant to this chapter. We emphasize that this research concentrated on the annual report and accounts. Data on all the other information that users place on their Investors Website was not included.

The financial section of the annual report and accounts

The most visited financial reporting information is the profit or loss account.

The notes to the accounts and the balance sheet come second.

The cash flow statement and the statement of total recognized gains and losses are among the least requested parts of the report.

The narrative section of the annual report and accounts

The most requested information is the remuneration report and the statement on compliance with the Combined Code for Corporate Governance. This research gives some insights as to what information users seek on the Internet but the results are dated and present activity may be different. Certainly, the amount and range of information on the websites has increased so one would expect there to be changes in the information of most interest to users.

eXtensible Business Reporting Language

XBRL converts printed financial statements into something that is computer readable. The benefits of using XBRL are claimed to be:

- For companies, cost savings and the streamlining of the collection and reporting of financial information.
- For investors, analysts, financial institutions, and regulators, they can find, compare, and analyze data more efficiently.
- The development of other taxonomies can be applied to a range of data including the management discussion and analysis, executive compensation, and sustainability reports.
- Improvement in the information efficiency in the capital markets.

Despite the claimed benefits of XBRL, there does not currently seem to be great enthusiasm to adopt it. A major questionnaire survey in the United Kingdom (Dunn, Heliar, Lymer, and Moussa 2013) found that key champions understand the advantages of XBRL but there is little understanding outside this group. The result is there is no effective use of the technology in the United Kingdom. Although the authors of the study put forward proposals for extending the use of XBRL, they believe that without greater regulatory commitment, XBRL will fade and die. However, our experience of corporate reporting on the Internet demonstrates that it can take several years before widespread adoption of a new technology. When this does occur, there is a large and rapid growth in its use. There are signs that digital or electronic reporting will become a fact.

Many countries have introduced electronic depositaries of financial statements to improve access. Some have also introduced the use of XBRL to tag data inside these reports to make smaller parts of the financial statement searchable and accessible.

The IFRS Foundation produces the IFRS Taxonomy in XBRL. It has also launched a research project to map current requirements for filing and the use of structured electronic filing around the world. The project is making progress and analysts undoubtedly will take advantage of these developments. The Financial Reporting Lab launched in 2014 is a project examining the impact technology might have on corporate reposting. The reason is that the volume of data generated by and about companies is increasing significantly and stakeholders need to understand these developments so that the advantages of technology could improve the effectiveness of corporate reports. The first report from the project was Digital Present released in 2015. This examined investors' views on the current state of digital corporate reporting by companies. The next stage of the project, entitled Digital Future, will investigate the impact of technology advancements on corporate reporting.

Beyond the Balance Sheet

Integrated Reporting

The International Integrated Reporting Council (IIRC) is a global coalition of regulators, investors, companies, standard setters, the accounting profession, and NGOs. The IASB and IIRC agreed to expand present corporate financial reporting to the level of integrated reporting which embraces accountability and stewardship. Such a report provides information on an organization's strategy, governance, performance, and prospects. The Integrated Reporting Model has identified six different capital inputs, but not all six may be appropriate for every company. International Integrated Reporting is designed to achieve the adoption of integrated reporting across the world thus

- Improve the quality of information available to providers of financial capital to enable a more efficient and productive allocation of capital.
- Promote a more cohesive and efficient approach to corporate reporting that draws on different reporting strands and communicates the full range of factors that materially affect the ability of an organization to create value over time.
- Enhance accountability and stewardship for the broad base of capitals (financial, manufactured, intellectual, human, social and relationship, and natural) and promote understanding of their independencies.

- Support integrated thinking, decision making, and actions that focus on the creation of value over the short, medium, and long term.

The IIRC published an explanatory IR framework in January 2021 to assist improved decision-useful reporting. The results are on its website www.integratedreporting.org/resource/international-ir-framework/.

Originally annual reports focused solely on financial information. Over the years the disclosures have grown so that there are usually at least three separate sections. Financial statements are a significant part but there may also be a management discussion and analysis, strategic reports, sustainability data governance disclosures, corporate governance, and other information that is not specifically financial. The 2007–2008 economic crisis revealed that financial reporting by itself does not provide sufficient information on short-term and long-term existence of a company.

The coalition is promoting communication about value creation as the next step in the evolution of corporate reporting. The first few words of its website states that integrated reporting has been created to "enhance accountability, stewardship and trust." Integrated reporting is now a leading practice in Japan and is part of the stock exchange listing rules in South Africa and Brazil.

The fundamental concepts of integrated reporting are concerned with the various capitals that the organization uses and affects, the organization's business model, and the creation of value over time. In using the word capital, the IIRC departs from the way that we use the term in financial accounting. Capital usually refers to equity, but the Integrated Reporting Model has identified six different capital inputs.

Financial capital:

funds obtained through financing, such as debt equity or grants, or generated through operations or investment

Manufacturing capital:

assets used for producing goods or providing services

Intellectual capital:

knowledge-based intangibles including intellectual property and organizational capital

Human capital:

people's competencies, capabilities, and experience; their motivations to innovate and their support for the organization's values

Social and relationship capital:

the institutions and the relationships within and between communities, groups of stakeholders, and other networks

Natural capital:

all renewable and nonrenewable environmental resources and processes that provide goods or services that support the past, current, or future prosperity of an organization

The IIRC has offered guiding principles and these are:

A. Strategic focus and future orientation
B. Connectivity of information
C. Stakeholder relationships
D. Materiality
E. Conciseness
F. Reliability and completeness
G. Consistency and comparability

We would add to this that the major firms of accountants are beginning to issue reports extolling the benefits of integrated reporting. It is too early to know whether the proposals will be successful but the actions by the EU and the proposals by the IIRC show where corporate reporting is moving: accountants are fully involved in these developments.

Sustainability (ESG)

ESG is an evaluation of a firm's collective conscientiousness for social and environmental factors. It is typically a score that is compiled from data collected surrounding specific metrics related to intangible assets within the enterprise. The question is whether sustainability is measurable and by whom. There are several groups, associations, and individuals interested in developing ESG. The European Corporate Reporting Lab @EFRAG was established by the European Financial Reporting Advisory Group (EFRAG) following the call by the European Commission (EC) in its

March 2018 Action Plan on financing sustainable growth. In the United States, the Office of the Federal Chief Sustainability Officer (CSO) is responsible for the development of policies, programs, and partnerships to promote sustainability. In 2021, the Biden–Harris Administration released plans developed by more than 20 federal agencies that outline the steps each agency will take to ensure their facilities and operations adapt to and are increasingly resilient to climate change.

The European Lab @EFRAG Project Task Force in 2021 published a report, "Towards Sustainable Businesses: Good Practices in Business Model, Risks and Opportunities Reporting in the EU" and supplementary document, "Supplementary Document: Good Reporting Practices."

There are many other initiatives concerned with sustainability or ESG. Many different terms are used in the literature and there is an abundance of acronyms. The actions and decisions being made are beyond the scope of this book, as sustainability is not a specific financial reporting issue but should be integrated with it.

In 2020, the IIRC and SASB announced their merger into the Value Reporting Foundation which would operate as one unified global organization. They argue that companies and investors have required more clarity and simplicity in corporate reporting. The merger should allow the new organization to support key bodies such as the IFRS Foundation. It should also be in a good position to cooperate with colleagues around the world and thus achieve a comprehensive corporate reporting system.

Although all the various organizations are attempting to address the issues of measuring and reporting sustainability by companies, there are many hurdles to be overcome. For example, despite many years of the development of international accounting, the United States and many other countries have not fully adopted international accounting. On a more local level, the question arises: Will the reporting of ESG by companies become the responsibility of accountants for approval and will this mean it is a subject to be studied by accounting students? There may also be the issue of "green washing." It is known that any disclosure of information may be affected by the giver who attempts to "white wash" the information. Will we enter into a situation where companies "green wash" their activities to persuade the users of the information that the company is actively ensuring sustainability?

Sustainability accounting and reporting cannot be implemented overnight; however, most companies that operate internationally should begin implementing sustainability reporting or they face the risk of falling behind. In December 2020, 80 percent of businesses worldwide had reported on sustainability (Threlfall *et al.* 2020). Recognizing climate risks is one example that an organization should begin integrating into their financial statements. According to the KPMG survey on sustainability it was found that North American countries are now leading the way in incorporating climate risks into their financial statements. A total of 58 percent of North American companies are reporting on the matter, followed by Asia Pacific at 45 percent, Europe at 41 percent, and lastly Middle East and Africa at 27 percent.

These figures indicate that this reporting practice is now a global trend and is here to stay. Companies which are transparent on the challenges they will face if changes are not made will assist management in getting these problems to the attention of the company's decision makers to identify ways to minimize these climate impacts.

One of the key challenges regarding sustainability reporting is that so far companies are encouraged to create these reports, but not mandated to do so. Making sustainable reporting mandatory has been a debate over the last 10 years as countries seem to have different opinions on the matter. We anticipate that this debate will continue for some years to come.

Conclusions

The ever-expanding growth in corporate reporting by companies may not be as beneficial as one would think. We may suffer from information overload! However, the main growth does not come from the requirements of International Financial Reporting Standards. Certainly, the regulations change but the actual amount of financial information that entities should disclose has not grown substantially.

The growth is in narrative reporting. We have strategic reports, sustainability reports, business models, governance, and stewardship as part of the printed annual report and accounts. In addition, companies understandably wish to communicate additional information about their successes, if not their failures. Much of the narrative information is not only directed to investors. It is noticeable that the FRC in some of its literature refers to stakeholders. There is a trend, backed in part by recent legislation, to demonstrate that a company is a good citizen. This takes us back to Chapter 1 and the debate on the users of corporate reports. It is now being acknowledged that other groups are interested in the activities of a company. The growth in the provision of nonfinancial information continues, as does the use of technology. It could be that these movements will bring about a measure of convergence in the annual report and accounts but still leave flexibility in disclosures for companies to satisfy the information needs of various users of corporate reports.

References

AAOIFI. 1999. *Accounting, Auditing and Governance Standards for Islamic Financial Institutions.* Manama.

Abdel-Khalik, A.R. 2019. "Failing Faithful Representations of Financial Statements: Issues in Reporting Financial Instruments." *Abacus* 55, no. 4. https://doi.org/10.1111/abac.12176

Adnan, M., and M. Gaffikin. 1997. "The Shari'a, Islamic Banks and Accounting Concepts and Practices." Paper presented at Accounting, Commerce and Finance: The Islamic Perspective International Conference, University of Western Sydney, Macarthur.

Ahmed, E. 1990. *Islamic Banking: Distribution of Profit.* Unpublished PhD Thesis, University of Hull.

Alexander, D., and E. Jermakowicz. June 2006. "A True and Fair View of the Rules and Principles Debate." *Abacus* 42, no. 2, pp. 132–164. 33p. https://doi.org/10.1111/j.1467-6281.2006.00195.x

Al-Amri, K., and M. Hossain. 2015. "A Survey of the Islamic Insurance Literature—Takaful." *Insurance Markets and Companies* 6, no. 1, pp. 53–61.

Ali, A.Y. 1992. *The Meaning of the Holy Qur'an, Commentary No. 324–326.* Amana Corporation, Brentwood, MD.

Anders, S.B. July 2015. "The Financial Reporting Council." *CPA Journal* 85, pp. 72–73.

Ashley, W.J. 1899. "The Commercial Legislation of England and the American Colonies, 1660–1760." *The Quarterly Journal of Economics.*

Askary, S., and F.L. Clarke. 1997. "Accounting in the Koranic Verses." Proceedings of the Conference on Accounting, Commerce and Finance: The Islamic Perspective, University of Western Sydney, pp. 18–20.

Atkins, P.S., and B.J. Bondi. 2008. "Evaluating the Mission: A Critical Review of the History and Evolution of the SEC Enforcement Program." *Fordham Journal Of Corporate & Financial Law* 13, no. 3, pp. 367–417.

Auerbach, A.J., M.P. Devereux, M. Keen, and J. Vella. 2017. "International Tax Planning under the Destination-Based Cash Flow Tax." *National Tax Journal* 70, no. 4.

Badua, F. December 2019. "Lies, Sex, and Suicide: Teaching Fundamental Accounting Concepts with Sordid Tales from the Seamier Side of Accounting History." *Accounting Historians Journal* 46, no. 2, pp. 53–59. 7p. https://doi.org/10.2308/aahj-52539

Baker, R. December 2017. "The Influence of Accounting Theory on the FASB's Conceptual Framework." *Accounting Historians Journal* 44, no. 2, pp. 109–124.

Balen, G. 2003. *The Secret History of the South Sea Bubble: The World's First Great Financial Scandal.*

Barker, R., and A. Teixeira. August 2018. "Gaps in the IFRS Conceptual Framework." *Accounting in Europe* 15, no. 2, pp. 153–166. 14p. https://doi .org/10.1080/17449480.2018.1476771.15

Barth, M., W. R. Landsman, M. Lang, and C. Williams. 2012. "Are International Accounting Standards-Based and US GAAP-Based Accounting Amounts Comparable?" *Journal of Accounting and Economics* 54, no. 1.

BEIS. 2019. "Audit Regime in the UK to be Transformed with New Regulator." www.gov.uk/government/news/audit-regime-in-the-uk-to-be-transformed-with-new-regulator

Belkaoui, A. 2000. *Accounting Theory.* London: International Thomson Business Press.

Bischof, J., and H. Daske. August 2016. "Interpreting the European Union's IFRS Endorsement Criteria: The Case of IFRS 9." *Accounting in Europe* 13, no. 2.

Black, D.E., T.E. Christensen, J.T. Ciesielski, and B.C. Whipple. 2018. "Non-GAAP Reporting: Evidence from Academia and Current Practice." *Journal of Business Finance Accounting* 45, pp. 259–294. HTTPS://DOI.ORG/10.1111/ jbfa.12298

Carnegie, G., and C. Napier. 2013. "Popular Accounting History: Evidence from Post Enron Stories." *Accounting Historians Journal* 40, no. 2.

Casabona, P.A., and T.G. Coville. 2018. "FASB's New Accounting Standard on Leases: Overview of Some Key Requirements for Lessees and Implementation Considerations." *Review of Business* 38, no. 1, pp. 59–73.

Chand, P., C. Patel, and R. Day. July 2008. "Factors Causing Differences in the Financial Reporting Practices in Selected South Pacific Countries in the Post Convergence Period." *Asian Academy of Management Journal* 13, no. 2, pp. 111–129.

Chandra, J.R., and M.R. Azam. January 2019. "Principles Verses Rules-Based Accounting Standards' Application in Fiji: An Overview of the Literature." *International Journal of Management, Accounting & Economics* 6, no. 1.

Chen G, and J. Zhou. 2019. "XBRL Adoption and Systematic Information Acquisition via EDGAR." *Journal of Information Systems.*

Cheng, C.S.A., P. Lin, J. Zhang, and S.B. Zhang. 2019. "IFRS Convergence and Stock Market Impact: Evidence from the 2007 China Reform." *Journal of Accounting & Finance (2158–3625)* 19, no. 9, pp. 30–45. 16p. https://doi .org/10.33423/jaf.v19i19.2694

Cheung, E., and J. Lau. 2016. "Readability of Notes to the Financial Statements and the Adoption of IFRS." *Australian Accounting Review* 26, no. 2, pp. 162–176.

Ciocan, C.C., and I. Georgescu. 2020. "The Perception of the Representatives of the Accounting Profession from Romania on the Relationship between Conservatism and True and Fair View." *Audit Financiar* 18, no. 159, pp. 585–598. 14p. https://doi.org/10.20869/AUDITF/2020/159/022

Clarke, F., R. Craig, and S. Hamid. 1996. "Physical Asset Valuation and Zakat: Insights and Implications." *Advances in International Accounting* 9, pp. 195–208.

Cohen, M.J. 1982. "Establishing Inflation Accounting Standards in the United States: A Developmental Process." *Journal of Comparative Corporate Law and Securities Regulation* 4, pp. 305–314. North-Holland Publishing Company.

Cohen, J.R., G. Krishnamoorthy, M. Peytcheva, and A.M. Wright. 2013. "How Does the Strength of the Financial Regulatory Regime Influence Auditors' Judgments to Constrain Aggressive Reporting in a Principles-Based Versus Rules-Based Accounting Environment?." *Accounting Horizons American Accounting Association* 27, no. 3, pp. 579–601. https://doi.org/10.2308/acch-50502

Colson, R.H. June 2005. "For Whom Do We Account?." *CPA Journal, 07328435* 75, no. 6.

Concepts and Standards Research Study Committee. 1964. "The Business Entity Concept." *Accounting Review.*

Craven, B.M., and C.L. Marston. 1999. "Financial Reporting on the Internet by Leading UK Companies." https://econpapers.repec.org) RePEc:taf:euract:v:8:y:19

De Luca, F., and J. PratherKinsey. 2018. "Legitimacy Theory May Explain the Failure of Global Adoption of IFRS: The Case of Europe and the U.S." *J Management* 22, pp. 501–534. https://doi.org/10.1007/s10997-018-9409-9

Dennis, I. 2019. "The Conceptual Framework—A 'Long and Winding Road'." *Accounting in Europe* 16, no. 3, pp. 256–289. https://doi.org/10.1080/1744 9480.2019.1624925

Driel, H. 2019. "Financial Fraud, Scandals, and Regulation: A Conceptual Framework and Literature Review." Business History 61, no. 8.

Dunn, T., C. Helliar, A. Lymer, and R. Moussa. 2013. "Stakeholder Engagement in International Financial Reporting." *The British Accounting Review* 45, pp. 167–182.

Ehsan, A., S. Saeed, M. Shahzad, and H. Iqbal. 2018. "Compliance of Financial Statements of Islamic Banks of Pakistan with AAOIFI Guidelines in General Presentation and Disclosure." *SEISENSE Journal of Management* 2, no. 1, pp. 12–21.

Elam, D. 2020. "Convergence Not: A Socieconomic Analysis of a Globalization Failure." *Journal of Applied Financial Research* 1, pp. 19–26.

Eng, L.L., and T. Vichitsarawong. 2017. "Usefulness of Accounting Estimates: A Tale of Two Countries (China and India)." *Journal of Accounting, Auditing & Finance* 32, no. 1, pp. 123–135.

Evans, L. 2003. "The True and Fair View and the Fair Override of IAS 1." *Accounting & Business Research* 33, no. 4, pp. 311–325. 15p. 1 Chart. https://doi.org/10.1080/00014788.2003.9729656

Faris, N. 1966. *The Mysteries of Almsgiving: A Translation from the Arabic of the Kitab Asrar al Zakah of Al-Ghazzali's Ihya "Ulum al-Din*, p. 8. Beirut: The American University of Beirut.

Financial Reporting Council. 2018. "UK Corporate Governance Code." www.frc.org.uk./directors/corporate-governance-and-stewardship/uk-corporate-governance-code

Fuad F., A. Juliarto, and P. Harto. 2019. "Does IFRS Convergence Really Increase Accounting Qualities?" *Emerging Market Evidence Journal of Economics, Finance and Administrative Science* 24, no. 48, pp. 205–220. https://doi.org/10.1108/JEFAS-10-2018-0099

Galbraith, K. 2009. *The Great Crash 1929*, Reprint ed. New York, NY: Mariner Books.

Gambling, T., and R.A.A. Karim. 1991. *Business and Accounting Ethics in Islam*. London: Mansell Publishing Limited.

Gornik-Tomaszewski, S., and Y.C. Choi. 2018. "The Conceptual Framework: Past, Present, and Future." *Review of Business* 38, no. 1, pp. 47–58.

Gray R., D. Owen, and K. Maunders. 1988. "Corporate Social Reporting: Emerging Trends in Accountability and Social Contract." *Accounting, Auditing and Accountability Journal* 1, no.1.

Hamat, M. January 1994. "The Accounting System in Islamic Banking." Conference on Interest-Free Banking Islamic Financial System, Malaysia.

Hancock, G.D., O.M.W. Sprague, and W.A. Scott. March 1912. *American Economic Review* 2, no. 1, pp. 125–132.

Haqiqi, A., and F. Pomeranz. 1987. "Accounting needs of Islamic banking." *Advances in International Accounting* 1, pp. 153–168.

Hassan, M.K., and S. Aliyu. 2018. "A Contemporary Survey of Islamic Banking Literature." *Journal of Financial Stability* 34, pp. 12–43.

Hassan, M.K., S. Aliyu, and M. Hussain. 2019. "A Contemporary Review of Islamic Finance and Accounting Literature." *The Singapore Economic Review.*

Homer, S. 1963. *A History of Interest Rates*. New Brunswick, Rutger University Press.

Hays, J.B., and D.L. Ariail. 2013. "Enron Should Not Have Been a Surprise and the Next Major Fraud Should Not Be Either." *Journal of Accounting & Finance (2158–3625)* 13, no. 3, pp. 134–145.

Henry, T.F., R.R. Weitz, and D.A. Rosenthal. February 2020. "The GAP Between GAAP and Non-GAAP." *CPA Journal* 90, no. 2, pp. 60–65. 6p.

Hoffmann, and Arden. 1983. "Legal Opinion Obtained by Accounting Standards Setting Committee." www.frc.org.uk/getattachment/afba0aa1-04fa-492a-beab-35918af6d97e/T-F-Opinon-13-September-1983.pdf

Hofstede, G.H. 1980. *Culture's Consequences, International Differences in Work Related Values.* Beverly Hills, CA: Sage Publications.

Hofstede, G. 1980–1981. "Culture and Organizations." *International Studies of Management & Organization,* Winter, 10, no. 4, pp. 15–41. 27p. https://doi.org/10.1080/00208825.1980.11656300 H

Istrate, C. 2015. "The Persistence of the Accounting Policies After the Transition to IFRS of the Romanian Listed Companies." *Accounting & Management Information Systems* 14, no. 4, pp. 599–626. 28p.

International Accounting Standards Board. 2007. IAS 1 *Presentation of Financial Statements.*

International Accounting Standards Board. 2003. *IAS 2 Inventories.*

International Accountings Standards Council. 1975. *IAS 1 The Presentation of Financial Statements.*

Jateaonkar, S.P., L. Lovata, and G.E. Sierra. 2014. "'U.S. GAAP versus IFRS' Analyst Forecast Errors for Private Financial Issuers." *Journal of Applied Financial Research* 2, pp. 9–19.

Kabir, H., and A. Rahman. 2018. "How Does the IASB Use the Conceptual Framework in Developing IFRSs? An Examination of the Development of IFRS 16 Leases." *Journal of Financial Reporting,* Fall, 3, no. 1, pp. 93–116. 24p. https://doi.org/10.2308/jfir-52232

Kirsch, R.J. June 2012. "The Evolution of the Relationship between the US Financial Accounting Standards Board and the International Accounting Standards Setters 1973-2008." *Accounting Historians Journal* 39, no. 1, pp. 1–51.

Kolton, P. March 1982. "The FASB in the 1980s: Standard Setting in a Changing Environment." *Journal of Accountancy* 153, no. 3, pp. 84–92. 6p.

Korok, R. 2018. "One Size Fits All? Costs and Benefits of Uniform Accounting Standards." *Journal of International Accounting Research American Accounting Association* 17, no. 1, pp. 1–23, Spring. https://doi.org/10.2308/jiar-51974

KPMG. 2011. "Corporate Sustainability: A Progress Report." Available at: www.KPMG.com (accessed December 15, 2016).

Krajňák, M. 2020. "Financial Statement according to National or International Financial Reporting Standards? A Decision Analysis Case Study from the Czech Republic at Industrial Companies." *Engineering Economics* 31, no. 3, pp. 270–281.

Kvaal, E. 2017. "The Role and Current Status of IFRS in the Completion of National Accounting Rules—Evidence from Norway." *Accounting in Europe* 14, nos. 1–2, 150–157. https://doi.org/10.1080/17449480.2017.1304646

Lee, T.A. 2006. "The FASB and Accounting for Economic Reality." *Accounting and the Public Interest* 6, pp. 1–21.

Macve, R. 1981. *A* Conceptual Framework For Financial Accounting and Reporting : The Possibilities for an Agreed Structure. Institute of Chartered Accountants in England and Wales.

Malone, L., A. Tarca, M. Wee, and S. Cahan. 2016. "IFRS Non-GAAP Earnings Disclosures and Fair Value Measurement." *Accounting and Finance* 56, pp. 59–97.

Marks R.A., and T.D. Jolicoeur. 2010. "The Fraud Files September/October." *The Value Examiner,* pp. 32–34.

Marsh, A., and R. Hussey. 1979. *Company Secretary's Review: Survey of Employee Reports.* Tolley.

Maurer, B. 2002. "Anthropological and Accounting Knowledge in Islamic Banking and Finance: Rethinking Critical Accounts." *Journal of the Royal Anthropological Institute* 8, no. 4, pp. 645–667.

May, G.O. 1943. *Financial Accounting: A Distillation of Experience.* Macmillan.

Mirza, M., and N. Baydoun. 1999. "Do Islamic Societies Need Their Own Accounting and Reporting Standards?." *Journal of the Academy of Business Administration* 4, no. 2, pp. 39–45.

Mirza, M., and N. Baydoun. 2000. "Accounting Policy in a Riba Free Environment." *Accounting, Commerce, and Finance: The Islamic Perspective Journal* 4, no. 1, pp. 30–40.

Miller, P.B.W., and P.R. Bahnson. October 2013. "FASB Finally Finds Freedom at 40." *Accounting Today,* pp. 14–15.

Napier, C. August 9–11, 2007. "Other Cultures, Other Accountings?" Islamic Accounting from past to present, 5th Accounting History International Conference, Banff, Canada.

Naylor, G. 1960. "Company Law for Shareholders." Hobart Paper No. 7. London: Institute of Economic Affairs.

Nelson, M. 2003. "Behavioural Evidence on the Effects of Principles and Rules Based Standards." *Accounting Horizons* 17, no. 1, pp. 91–104.

Norby, W. May/June 1980. "Inflation Accounting." *Great Britain Financial Analysts Journal* 36, no. 3, pp. 17–80. 3p.

Pollanen, R.M. 2020. "Public Sector Accounting Standards Conundrum in Canada And United States: National Vs International Standards." *International Journal of Business, Accounting, and Finance* 14, no. 1, Spring, pp. 142–159.

PWC. 2010. "Open to Comparison: Islamic Finance and IFRS." PWC series paper.

Robson, K. 1994. "Inflation Accounting and Action at a Distance: The Sandilands Episode." *Accounting, Organizations and Society* 19, no. 1, pp. 45–82.

Rowbottom, N., A. Allam, and A. Lymer. 2005. "Exploring the Use and Users of Narrative Reporting in the Online Annual Report." *Journal of Applied Accounting Research* 11, no. 2, pp. 90–108.

Sangster, A. 2016. "The Genesis of Double Entry Bookkeeping." *The Accounting Review* 91, no. 1, pp. 299–315.

Sangster, A. March 2018. "Pacioli's Lens: God, Humanism, Euclid, and the Rhetoric of Double Entry." *Accounting Review* 93, no. 2, pp. 299–314. 16p. 2 Charts. https://doi.org/10.2308/accr-51850

Schneider, E., M. Morys, M. Lampe, and K. Enflo. August 2017. "Review of Periodical Literature on Continental Europe from 1700 published in 2013." Economic History Review, *Economic History Society* 70, no. 3, pp. 1–45.

Shahul, H., and R. Yaya. July 28–29, 2003. "The Future of Islamic Corporate Reporting: Lessons from Alternative Western Accounting Reports." *The International Conference on Quality Financial Reporting and Corporate Governance.*

Shihadah, S. 1987. *Financial Accounting Theory From Islamic Perspective.* Cairo: AlZahraa for Arabic Media. [Arabic].

Siddiqi, S. 1982. *Public Finance in Islam.* Delhi: Adam Publishers.

Spalding, A.D., Jr., and G.R. Lawrie. 2019. "A Critical Examination of the AICPA's New 'Conceptual Framework'." *Ethics Protocol J Bus Ethics* 155, pp. 1135–1152. DOI 10.1007/s10551-017-3528-0

Sprouse, R.T., and M.A. Moonitz. 1962. "A Tentative Set of Broad Accounting Principles for Business Enterprises." American Institute of Certified Business Accountants.

Taggart, H. July 1953. "Sacred Cows in Accounting." *The Accounting Review,* pp. 315–316.

Tamimi, N., and R. Sebastianelli. n.d. "Transparency Among S&P 500 Companies: An Analysis of ESG Disclosure Scores."

Trade Union Research Unit. 1981. *Working in Britain.* Ruskin College.

Triyuwono, I. 2000. "Shari'a Accounting: Implementation of Justice in a Form of Trust Metaphor." *Journal of Accountancy and Auditing* 4, no. 1, pp. 1–34. Indonesia.

Vasile, E., and I. Croitoru. December 2020. "Financial Statements—Object of the Financial Audit." *Internal Auditing & Risk Management,* no. 4, pp. 51–58. 8p.

Violet, W., and J.D. Hansen. 2013. "Abstractions in Accounting (The Accounting Problem)." *Journal of Theoretical Accounting Research* 9, no. 1, pp. 108–114. 7p. Fall.

Walton, P. August 2018. "Discussion of Barker and Teixeira ([2018]. Gaps in the IFRS Conceptual Framework. Accounting in Europe, 15) and Van Mourik and Katsuo ([2018]. Profit or loss in the IASB Conceptual Framework.

Accounting in Europe, 15).” *Accounting in Europe* 15, no. 2, pp. 193–199. 7p.

Whittington, G. June 2008. “Fair Value and the IASB/FASB Conceptual Framework Project: An Alternative View.” *Abacus* 44, no. 2, pp. 139–168. 30p.

Whittington, G. 2015. “Measurement in Financial Reporting: Half a Century of Research and Practice.” *ABACUS* 51, no. 4.

Whyte, M.J.A. 2017. “A U.S. Imperative: High Quality, Globally Accepted Accounting Standards.” www.sec.gov.news/statementwhite-2016-01-05.html

Widman, M. November 19, 1994. *Daimler's NYSE Listing Piques German Interest.* New York Times.

Yamey, B. July 1994. “Accounting in History.” *European Accounting Review* 3, no. 2, pp. 375–380. 6p.

Zaid, O. 1995. *Financial Accounting in Islamic Society.* Amman: Dar Al-Yazouri. [Arabic].

Zeff, S., and C. Nobes. 2010. “Has Australia or Any Other Jurisdiction Adopted IFRS.” *Australian Accounting Review* 20, no. 2, pp. 178–184. doi. org/10.1111/j.1825-2561

About the Authors

Roger Hussey, PhD, MSc, FCCA, is a fellow of the Association of Chartered Certified Accountants and received his MSc in Industrial Relations and his PhD in Financial Communications from the University of Bath, United Kingdom. He has taught in Australia, Canada, China, and the United Kingdom. Roger is the author of nearly 40 books. Roger worked in industry for several years before moving to the Industrial Relations Unit at St Edmund Hall, Oxford University, as Director of Research into Employee Communications. He was later appointed as Deloitte and Touche Professor of Financial Reporting at the University of the West of England. Roger was previously Dean of the Odette School of Business and is now Professor Emeritus at the University of Windsor, Canada, and the University of the West of England.

Talal Al-Hayale, PhD, MA, received his MA in Finance and his PhD in Accounting from the University of Wales, United Kingdom. He has taught in England, Canada, China, and Jordan. Talal is the author or co-author of more than 30 articles published in the United States, the United Kingdom, and the Middle East. Talal worked as an advisor to several banks in the Middle East. He is currently a professor at the University of Windsor in Canada.

Index

OTHER TITLES IN THE FINANCIAL ACCOUNTING COLLECTION

Mark Bettner, Bucknell University, and
Michael Coyne, Fairfield University, Editors

- *A Guide to the New Language of Accounting and Finance* by Hussey Roger and Ong Audra
- *International Auditing Standards in the United States* by Asokan Anandarajan and Gary Kleinman
- *Twenty-First Century Corporate Reporting* by Gerald Trites
- *Calling Out COVID-19* by Faisal Sheikh, Nigel Iyer, Brian Leigh and Geetha Rubasundram
- *Accounting for Business* by Roger Hussey and Audra Ong
- *Tax Aspects of Corporate Division* by W. Eugene Seago
- *When Numbers Don't Add Up* by Faisal Sheikh
- *Sustainability Performance and Reporting* by Irene M. Herremans
- *Applications of Accounting Information Systems* by David M. Shapiro
- *A Non-Technical Guide to International Accounting* by Roger Hussey and Audra Ong
- *Forensic Accounting and Financial Statement Fraud, Volume I* by Zabihollah Rezaee
- *Forensic Accounting and Financial Statement Fraud, Volume II* by Zabihollah Rezaee

Concise and Applied Business Books

The Collection listed above is one of 30 business subject collections that Business Expert Press has grown to make BEP a premiere publisher of print and digital books. Our concise and applied books are for...

- Professionals and Practitioners
- Faculty who adopt our books for courses
- Librarians who know that BEP's Digital Libraries are a unique way to offer students ebooks to download, not restricted with any digital rights management
- Executive Training Course Leaders
- Business Seminar Organizers

Business Expert Press books are for anyone who needs to dig deeper on business ideas, goals, and solutions to everyday problems. Whether one print book, one ebook, or buying a digital library of 110 ebooks, we remain the affordable and smart way to be business smart. For more information, please visit www.businessexpertpress.com, or contact sales@businessexpertpress.com.

www.ingramcontent.com/pod-product-compliance
Lightning Source LLC
Chambersburg PA
CBHW061323220326
41599CB00026B/5010